Scaling, Innovation &
Success In Entrepreneurship

DARE TO DREAM BIG

ADRIANA LUNA CARLOS

KLARA REID I EDWINA ADAMS I DARLENE OLIVER
ELIZABETH COREY I GEMMA BULOS I JOAHNA TUPAS

ISBN: 978-1-960136-76-3

Table of Contents

INTRODUCTION

Are you one of the many visionaries out there, fueled by the fire of innovation, eager to transform your dreams into tangible success stories? Whether you're just stepping into the world of entrepreneurship or you've been navigating its intricate paths for years, one truth remains constant: the journey is riddled with challenges, uncertainties, and the relentless pursuit of growth.

"Dare To Dream Big" is not just another book on business; it's a roadmap designed to navigate the twists and turns of entrepreneurial ventures. Within these pages lies a treasure trove of insights, strategies, and wisdom garnered from the trenches of entrepreneurship.

Through these women's own journey of awakening, they emerge as beacons of change, offering solutions to restore physical and mental health. With their chronicles, they urge readers to embrace and unlock their innate healing potential. Their message resonates with authenticity and genuine empathy, offering a guiding light for women navigating life's complexities. They encourage readers to embrace their own journeys with courage and determination, knowing that their adversities can ultimately become their greatest strengths. Through their unwavering optimism and resilience, readers are inspired to become NOISE-makers in their own lives, turning adversity into a narrative of inspiration and empowerment. Prepare to be challenged and empowered as our women dreamers share their remarkable stories and advocate for a healthier and meaningful world.

Adriana Luna Carlos

Founder and CEO of She Rises Studios & FENIX TV

https://www.linkedin.com/in/adriana-luna-carlos/
https://www.facebook.com/adrianalunacarlos
https://www.instagram.com/sherisesstudios_llc/
https://www.sherisesstudios.com/
https://www.srslatina.com/
https://fenixtv.app/

Adriana Luna Carlos is an accomplished web and graphic designer, author, and mentor with a passion for helping women succeed in life and business. With over 10 years of experience in graphic and web arts, Adriana has built a reputation as an innovative leader and entrepreneur. In 2020, she co-founded She Rises Studios, a multi-digital media company and publishing house that has helped countless clients achieve their branding and marketing goals. In 2023, she co-created FENIX TV, an online streaming platform that showcases stories of people breaking barriers, shattering stereotypes, and triumphing against the odds.

As an advocate for women's success, Adriana challenges her clients and mentees to strive for nothing less than excellence. She has a deep understanding of the insecurities and challenges that women often face in the business world and provides the guidance and resources needed to overcome them. Her success as a business leader and entrepreneur has made her a sought-after mentor and speaker at events around the world.

Through her work, Adriana has demonstrated a commitment to creating opportunities for women to succeed in business and life. Her passion for innovation, leadership, and women's empowerment has made her a respected figure in the business community, and her impact will undoubtedly continue to inspire and empower women for years to come.

DREAMS ARE EVOLVING BLUEPRINTS

By Adriana Luna Carlos

"The future belongs to those who believe in the beauty of their dreams." —Eleanor Roosevelt

This quote is simple but incredibly powerful. However, I see more than just the beauty in our dreams; I see endless possibilities, the sparks of innovation, the joy of collaboration, and the potential for growth. It's thrilling to dream big, to imagine and talk about what we want without letting fear get in the way. Always remember to push aside any doubts and really listen to what your dreams are telling you.

As an entrepreneur, I've found that believing in the beauty of my dreams is the key to turning them into reality. From a young age, I was fascinated by the idea that with enough passion and determination, anything is possible. This belief led me to co-found She Rises Studios, a place where we aim to empower women and promote diversity. Our goal is to help women conquer their insecurities, realize their leadership potential, and dare to dream big.

Starting in high school with a passion for graphic communications, and then founding my own company at 18, my journey has always been driven by big dreams and the pursuit of making them real. The ups and downs I've faced along the way have only strengthened my conviction that dreaming big is essential. Now, as one of the CEOs of She Rises Studios, I continue to dream big and inspire others to do the same.

This book, "Dare To Dream Big," is a reflection of that belief. It's meant to be a guide, a resource, and a source of inspiration for entrepreneurs at any stage. Whether you're just starting out or looking to grow your business, this book offers practical advice, strategies, and insights to help you through the challenges of entrepreneurship. By believing in the beauty of our dreams and daring to dream big, we can transform our lives and the world around us.

Early Beginnings

I always think that I stumbled into something amazing when I went to sign up for the Graphics Communication Academy (GCA). I knew some of what we would potentially get into, but what I didn't know was how much it would change the trajectory of my life and how many new doors it would open. At that time, I loved computers but was still such a novice. The prospect of using those "new" Apple computers was thrilling. This is where my love for Apple would grow.

I went in with a friend as she signed up for the Visual Arts & Design Academy (VADA), but I knew I couldn't draw at all. So, I took a leap and went into a program where I felt I more belonged, even though it meant I wouldn't know anyone. This was a commitment because it was a three-year program at my high school. Most teenagers barely know what they want to eat, let alone make a three-year commitment so rashly. But this is who I was and who I am. I've always been someone who dives into the deep end without fearing the "what ifs." I was excited to overcome obstacles because I loved a challenge.

One of my favorite experiences was getting to design a logo and card for a previous alumni reunion. It was either their 40th or 50th reunion, and a group of elderly alumni came into our class. They looked so amazed and excited to see our class and to know what the future had turned into. I remember feeling so lucky to be a part of their history. I was second in this "competition"; they ended up selecting another design, but this only fueled me more!

My teacher was pretty cool. She always showed us her artwork from projects outside of class to give us a glimpse of "real world experiences."

She didn't treat us like students; she treated us as colleagues. We got to do fun projects that mixed design with a sense of ownership and entrepreneurship. She taught us how to make products like t-shirts, school newspapers, and even how to create pitches, websites, resumes, and cover letters. It was a future entrepreneur's dream. I felt so at home and inspired daily.

Taking the Leap

I was motivated to start my own design business at 18 because I noticed how people were hiring graphic designers at astronomical rates for work that often looked subpar. I wanted to show myself that I could rise to the challenge, make some side money in college, and be independent. The idea was thrilling at the time.

I began by placing ads on Craigslist, offering services for logo design, brochures, flyers, and business cards. My prices were low since I was still fresh in the field. This venture taught me how to communicate with strangers, negotiate deals, and market my skills realistically while still exuding confidence. It was scary but also incredibly fun!

However, I faced significant challenges. Many customers doubted my abilities due to my age and gender. Some tried to take advantage of me, assuming I would back down easily. But I always stood my ground and let my work speak for itself.

Navigating Challenges

Handling financial challenges and resource constraints was one of the biggest hurdles. I had limited funds and no formal business training. I had to learn everything on the fly—how to budget, manage time, and balance my personal life with the demands of running a business. There were moments of doubt and fear, but I pushed through by focusing on my passion for design and the satisfaction of delivering quality work.

One particular challenge was balancing college coursework with client deadlines. There were nights when I barely slept, juggling design projects and studying for exams. But each completed project and satisfied client reinforced my belief in my capabilities and motivated me to keep going.

Successes and Milestones

Despite the challenges, there were many early successes that validated my efforts. One of my first big breaks came when a local restaurant hired me to design their entire branding package. Seeing my designs come to life in menus, signage, and advertisements around town was immensely rewarding.

A specific achievement that made me particularly proud was winning a design competition for a community event. My work was chosen out of several entries, and it was displayed prominently at the event. This recognition boosted my confidence and opened up more opportunities.

These early successes had a significant impact on my future entrepreneurial endeavors. They taught me the importance of perseverance, self-belief, and the value of hard work. They also showed me that age and gender do not define one's ability to succeed in business. These lessons became the foundation of my approach to entrepreneurship and set the stage for my later work with She Rises Studios.

Transitioning to She Rises Studios

Between running my own graphic design and website design company at 18 and co-founding She Rises Studios, there was a journey filled with obstacles, setbacks, failures, and losses. But through it all, I never lost my spark, drive, or commitment to impact those around me. While others may have become jaded, I held onto hope and continued to believe in the possibility of making a difference.

She Rises Studios emerged as a new opportunity to channel my passion on a larger scale and to impact lives that were receptive to being empowered. My past experiences profoundly influenced my approach to running She Rises Studios. With a wealth of practical knowledge and experience under my belt, I was better equipped to navigate the challenges of entrepreneurship and understand the psychology of business. This enabled me to connect more effectively with clients, anticipate their needs, and communicate with them in a way that resonated.

At the heart of She Rises Studios is a vision of collaboration, celebration, and upliftment. We envisioned a space where individuals could come together to support one another and celebrate each other's successes. For me, business has always been about more than just making a profit; it's about making a positive impact on people's lives. That guiding principle has shaped everything we do at She Rises Studios, from our mission to our values and the way we interact with our community.

My Truth of Entrepreneurship

Being an entrepreneur is more than just starting a business; it's about embodying a mindset of innovation, resilience, and vision. My identity as an entrepreneur is deeply rooted in my commitment to these values. I strive to create a positive impact through my work and empower others to do the same.

The path to success is rarely smooth. My journey has been filled with both failures and triumphs, each offering valuable lessons. Early on, I faced financial difficulties, self-doubt, and the constant pressure to succeed. However, these experiences taught me the importance of perseverance and adaptability. Every setback became a stepping stone, propelling me closer to my goals.

Dare To Dream Big

The idea for "Dare To Dream Big" emerged from my desire to share the collective wisdom of successful entrepreneurs. I wanted to create a resource that would inspire and guide others on their entrepreneurial journeys. This book is a testament to the power of dreaming big and the impact it can have on one's life and business.

I felt a distinct absence of a collective voice, particularly one driven by the passion and commitment of women entrepreneurs like those featured in our anthology. I wanted this book to not only exist but to thrive within a community of women who share a deep dedication to their own success and to uplifting others. The women in this book are not just sharing their stories; they're baring their souls, offering raw truths, and providing a roadmap to their achievements, both present and future.

Scaling, innovation, and success are not just buzzwords; they're the essence of entrepreneurship. While these concepts may seem straightforward on the surface, delving into each reveals layers of complexity and nuance. Scaling involves strategic growth, innovation requires creativity and adaptability, and success is a multifaceted journey marked by triumphs and challenges. Understanding and mastering these core elements are crucial for navigating the ever-evolving landscape of entrepreneurship.

My overarching goal for "Dare To Dream Big" is to empower readers with a multifaceted toolkit for success. I want readers to gain not only perspective and insight but also practical steps, tools, emotional intelligence, and the inspiration needed to embark on their own entrepreneurial journey. This book is more than just a collection of stories; it's a beacon of guidance and motivation for anyone daring to dream big in the world of entrepreneurship.

Scaling in Entrepreneurship

Scaling is crucial in entrepreneurship—it's about growing your business while keeping it efficient and profitable. Scaling strategies are key whether you're starting out or aiming to push your existing business further.

Scaling lets you expand your business, tap into new markets, and boost revenue. It helps you make the most of what you have, improving efficiency and staying competitive. Strategic scaling sets you up for lasting success and value.

Approaching Scaling

When you're considering scaling your business, there are several important steps to take. First, take a close look at your business's current state. Evaluate how things are running, what resources you have available, and where you stand in the market. Assess whether you're ready to grow by considering factors such as the demand for your products or services, your financial performance, and your team's capacity to handle additional work.

Next, it's essential to set clear growth goals for your business. Determine what you want your business to achieve and where you want it to go. This could involve expanding into new markets, increasing production, or diversifying your product offerings. Setting specific goals helps you plan the necessary steps to make your business bigger and better.

Understanding your market is also crucial when approaching scaling. Take the time to research your market thoroughly to identify growth opportunities and understand your customers' needs. Analyze industry trends, study your competitors, and gain insights into what your customers like and dislike about your products or services.

As you plan for growth, it's important to prepare for potential challenges that may arise along the way. Anticipate what could go wrong and have contingency plans in place to address these challenges. This might involve setting aside extra funds for emergencies or developing strategies to mitigate operational risks.

Lastly, aim for sustainability as you scale your business. Growing too quickly can sometimes lead to problems down the line. It's essential to maintain the quality of your products or services and prioritize customer satisfaction, even as your business expands. Keep your long-term vision in mind and ensure that your growth strategy aligns with your values and goals.

Is Scaling Right for You? Scaling isn't the best choice for every business. It depends on things like what you do, how the market is doing, and what your business can handle. Think about how your business works, what you've got to work with, and if making it bigger fits with what you want to do.

Is Your Business Ready to Grow?

Use this checklist to assess if your business is ready to take the next step and grow!

Step 1: Check Your Business Basics

- Look at how your business is doing right now: Are you making enough sales? Are you able to cover your expenses?

- Figure out if people want what you're selling: Do you have customers who keep coming back? Are you getting new customers interested in your products/services?

- Make sure you're making enough money to grow: Is your business making a profit? Do you have some extra money to invest in growing your business?

- Think about whether your team can handle more work: Do you have enough people to help you if your business gets busier?

Step 2: Set Your Growth Goals

- Decide what you want your business to do next: Do you want to sell more products/services? Do you want to reach new customers in different areas?

- Choose areas where you want to get bigger: Are there specific parts of your business you want to expand, like your product line or the number of locations?

- Make clear goals for what you want to achieve: Can you set specific targets, like increasing sales by a certain percentage or launching a new product by a certain date?

Step 3: Understand Your Market

- Find out more about the people who buy from you: Who are your customers? What do they like about your products/services?

- See what other businesses like yours are doing: Are there competitors offering similar products/services? What are they doing well?

- Learn about what's popular and what's not in your industry: Are there trends in your industry that you can take advantage of? Are there any changes in customer preferences or buying habits?

Step 4: Plan Your Resources

- Think about what you need to grow (like money and people): Do you have enough resources to support your growth plans? Do you need to invest in new equipment or hire more staff?

- Decide how you'll use what you have to get bigger: Can you make better use of your existing resources to support your growth goals?

- Get ready for things that might go wrong along the way: Are there any risks or challenges you need to prepare for, like unexpected expenses or changes in the market?

Step 5: Make Sure You Can Keep Up

- Make sure your business can handle getting bigger: Are your operations and processes scalable? Can you handle an increase in sales volume or customer inquiries?

- Find ways to make things run smoother: Are there any inefficiencies or bottlenecks in your business that you can address to improve efficiency?

- Make sure you're growing in a way that's good for the long run: Are you prioritizing sustainable growth practices that won't compromise the quality of your products/services or customer satisfaction?

Step 6: Decide if Scaling is Right for You

- Look at everything you've figured out: Based on your assessment, does it seem like your business is ready to grow?

- Think about whether growing your business is the best choice for you: Are the potential benefits of scaling worth the investment and effort required?

- Make a plan for how you'll make it happen if you decide to go for it: Can you outline specific steps and milestones for achieving your growth goals?

Innovation in Entrepreneurship:

Innovation isn't just about inventing new stuff; it's about finding fresh ways to solve problems, create value, and stay ahead in business. As an entrepreneur, being creative can help you stand out and grow your business. I want to show you how being creative, adapting to change, and coming up with new ideas can help your business succeed.

Being creative means thinking of new ideas and doing things in different ways. It's about being original and thinking outside the box. For entrepreneurs, being creative can help you come up with cool products, awesome marketing, or better ways to run your business. It's like being an artist—using your imagination to make something amazing.

In business, things are always changing. Being able to adapt means being flexible and able to change your plans when needed. It's like being a superhero—able to handle whatever comes your way and turn challenges into opportunities. Being adaptable helps you stay relevant and keep your business moving forward.

Innovation is about turning your ideas into something real that makes a difference. It's about taking your cool ideas and making them into products or services that people want. For entrepreneurs, innovation means listening to your customers, trying new things, and working with others to make your ideas come to life. It's like being a problem solver—finding new and better ways to do things.

Is Your Business Innovating Yet?

Here are some friendly nudges to help spark innovation in your business. Feel free to pick one or try them all—whatever suits your business's values and your dreams:

1. **Unleash Your Inner Creator**: Are you tinkering and toying with fresh ideas to jazz up your products or services?

2. **Embrace Adaptability**: Can you quickly adjust your strategies and approaches when faced with unexpected challenges or changes in the market?

3. **Seek Out "Aha!" Moments**: Do you ever find yourself sniffing around for spots in your business where a little innovation could sprinkle some magic?

4. **Team Up and Tag Along**: Are you throwing a brainstorm party, inviting all your team members to jump in and cook up some genius ideas together?

5. **Keep Score of Your Wins**: Are you high-fiving yourself for the ways your innovative moves are making waves in your business?

6. **Never Stop Polishing the Gem**: Are you on a never-ending quest to spruce up your business, adding a dash of sparkle here and a dollop of shine there?

Innovation isn't just a fancy word—it's the fuel that keeps your business engine running smoothly. So, whether you're trying out new ideas, rolling with the punches, or celebrating your wins, keep innovating and watch your business grow!

Achieving Success in Entrepreneurship

Defining Success Success isn't just about hitting a particular target; it's about finding fulfillment in what you do and leaving a positive impact. For me, success means growing personally and professionally while helping others do the same. It's about inspiring and guiding your team, setting clear goals, and creating a work environment where everyone can thrive. Building a strong team is essential too—surround yourself with people who share your vision and bring out the best in each other.

Setting clear goals is essential for success in entrepreneurship. It's like having a roadmap for your journey, guiding you toward your destination. By knowing where you want to go and how to get there, you can stay focused and on track, even when faced with challenges.

Commitment is key in the entrepreneurial journey. Success doesn't happen overnight; it requires dedication and perseverance. Like tending to a garden, you need to nurture your goals and keep working toward them, no matter what obstacles arise.

Seeking mentorship is valuable for aspiring entrepreneurs. It's like having a trusted guide who can offer advice and support based on their own experiences. Mentors provide insights and encouragement, helping you navigate the ups and downs of entrepreneurship with confidence.

The Success Spectrum

Since success means something different to everyone I wanted to share another way to visualize this where each step towards entrepreneurial success is represented by a different color. We can visualize it as a journey from dreaming big to achieving milestones, with each color representing a different aspect of success.

1. Dream Big Yellow: This color represents the starting point of every entrepreneurial journey—believing in the beauty of your dreams and daring to dream big. It's about envisioning what you want to achieve and setting ambitious goals to make it happen.

2. Commitment Crimson: As entrepreneurs, commitment is crucial. This shade symbolizes the dedication and persistence needed to overcome obstacles and stay focused on your goals, even when faced with challenges.

3. Mentorship Mint: Seeking mentorship is like adding a refreshing boost to your entrepreneurial journey. This minty

hue represents the guidance and support you receive from experienced mentors who help you navigate the ups and downs of entrepreneurship.

4. Innovation Indigo: Innovation is the lifeblood of entrepreneurship, and this deep indigo shade captures its essence. It's about thinking outside the box, embracing creativity, and finding fresh ways to solve problems and create value in your business.

5. Scaling Sage: Scaling your business is a strategic move towards growth and expansion. This serene sage color symbolizes the careful planning and execution required to take your business to the next level while maintaining efficiency and profitability.

6. Success Sunset: Finally, we have the vibrant hues of success, resembling the glow of a beautiful sunset after a long day's journey. Success in entrepreneurship is about achieving personal and professional fulfillment, making a positive impact, and celebrating your milestones along the way.

By visualizing success as a spectrum of colors, we can see that each step of the entrepreneurial journey contributes to the overall picture of success. Whether you're dreaming big, committing to your goals, seeking mentorship, innovating, scaling your business, or celebrating your successes, each color adds its unique hue to the canvas of entrepreneurship. Make these colors what you want, define your OWN success story and share it with the world.

Dare To Dream Big

Dreaming big is not just about achieving grandiose goals; it's about believing in the potential within yourself and your business. By embracing the ideas of scaling, innovation, and success, you can transform your entrepreneurial journey and create lasting impact.

I encourage you to take the first step towards your entrepreneurial dreams. Whether you're starting a new venture or seeking to grow an existing business, remember that the future belongs to those who believe in the beauty of their dreams. **Dare to dream big**, and the path to entrepreneurial success awaits.

As my chapter comes to a close, I'm excited to pass the baton to the incredible women whose stories await you in the following pages. Each of them brings a unique perspective, a wealth of experience, and a passion for making a difference. So, let their voices inspire you, let their stories ignite your imagination, and remember, dreams are evolving blueprints. They shape our journey, guide our actions, and lead us toward the futures we envision.

Joahna Tupas

School in a Backpack LLC
Founder and Chief Consultant

https://www.linkedin.com/in/joahnatupas/
https://www.facebook.com/joahnatupas
https://www.instagram.com/joahnatupas
www.schoolinabackpack.com
https://youtube.com/@joahnatupas

Joahna Tupas is a highly respected figure in experiential and character education, having been featured in prominent publications like CEO Weekly, Who's Who of Professional Women, and Millennium Magazine. In 2004, she founded her Multimedia Arts Production Company during college, aiming to revolutionize the freelancing landscape in the Philippines. Through strategic collaborations with industry peers, her company quickly gained recognition among top-tier clients. Transitioning into academia, Joahna brought her wealth of industry expertise to the classroom, becoming a respected college professor. Embracing motherhood, she embarked on a new chapter as a worldschooling parent, prioritizing experiential learning and character development for her son. When not engaged in public speaking, writing, or pursuing her passions such as dancing, rapping, or surfing, Joahna focuses on empowering parents, educators, and learners through self-awareness and intentional living. To discover more about Joahna Tupas and her mission to inspire purposeful courage in passionate pursuits, visit www.schoolinabackpack.com.

THE COURAGE TO BEGIN AGAIN: DEBUNKING BIZ MYTHS FOR FRESH STARTS AND POSSIBILITIES

By Joahna Tupas

"I'm back at square one," I muttered, gazing at the myriad of business ideas gathering dust on my shelf. Let's dive into a candid conversation about something we know too well: frustration.

How many times have we poured our hearts and souls into a business plan, only to watch it fizzle out? How often do we feel like we're drowning in a sea of expectations, struggling to keep our heads above water? And don't even get me started on the feeling of defeat when ideas fail to take off! It's enough to make you want to throw in the towel.

Well, I've been there, done that. I've felt the sting of disappointment and the weight of unmet expectations.

And you know what? It's okay to feel that way. Trust me, I've been in those shoes more times than I can count. It's all part of the journey.

Meet the BohoChic

Let's peek behind the curtain of my current adventure. Picture this: I'm humbly adorned with the titles of international speaker, bestselling author, and life coach. It's a whirlwind of excitement, that's for sure.

As I traverse from one stage to another as an international speaker, my mission is to inspire, empower, and encourage audiences wherever I go. And let me tell you, there's something truly magical about seeing eyes light up as I share stories and practical insights that can be put into action.

But that's not all. Being a bestselling author? It's like living in a dream world. Every time I see my words resonating with readers, it's a pinch-me moment.

In my role as a life coach, the real magic happens as I guide individuals to uncover their passions, conquer obstacles, and step into their fullest potential as they discover themselves.

It's a privilege I don't take lightly and never take for granted.

It's hard to believe how far I've come. I dipped my toes into the entrepreneurial world while still in college, two years before earning my bachelor's degree. Back then, Multimedia Arts was a relatively new course, not as widely recognized or utilized as it is today. Yet I saw its potential and wanted to get a head start on my post-grad career by building an industry portfolio. It was challenging.

Companies were hesitant to hire an undergrad with limited experience. As a freelancer with the right qualifications, I encountered firsthand the prevalent stereotype of being undervalued and overworked in the industry. I recognized the untapped potential of freelancers and their invaluable flexibility and creativity and set out to revolutionize the freelancing industry. As a junior, I launched my multimedia arts production company long before platforms like Upwork and Fiverr gained prominence.

With my close-knit college friends as my initial crewmates, our company experienced rapid growth, attracting a diverse array of freelancers, both novices and seasoned professionals. In just a short period, our clientele expanded from private individuals to internationally recognized companies and brands, solidifying our position in the industry.

Between then and now, my journey has been a whirlwind of twists and turns, filled with unexpected opportunities and invaluable lessons. Adapting to change has become second nature—I've learned that life is all about evolving and seizing new chances as they come. Like a seasoned traveler exploring uncharted waters, I've ventured through various roles and industries, always eager for the next adventure.

I dove headfirst into the publishing realm, first as a marketing assistant, and immersed myself in design, photography, eventually securing a position as a managing editor. My hunger for new experiences led me to explore the vibrant world of art exhibits and music gigs, curating several events to showcase talented artists throughout the country.

As I delved into the events industry, my initial gig of snapping photos and shooting videos soon grew into something bigger. I found myself co-orchestrating some pretty impressive commemorative events, including some fancy ones at the Malacañan Palace—you know, like the White House, but Filipino-style, complete with VIP politicians mingling in the crowd.

Then came the digital revolution, and I found myself riding the social media wave, working in marketing, PR, and consultancy for major players in Singapore, Sydney, and San Francisco. My passion for sustainability also burned bright—I co-directed an architectural competition that made waves with an exhibit at the Massachusetts Institute of Technology.

When it came to education, I focused on revolutionizing the norms and leaving a meaningful mark. This drive led me to advocate for experiential learning and character education, spearheading groundbreaking initiatives such as worldschooling—educating children through travel, exposing them to diverse cultures and environments for hands-on learning experiences—in the Philippines.

Shifting into the education sector has been an immensely rewarding part of my journey. Initially invited to become a college professor due to my industry background, this journey later led me to teaching in community and international schools. Eventually, I seized the chance to move to the USA, where I now contribute as the Founder and Chief Consultant of School in a Backpack LLC, supporting families and educators alike.

Throughout my journey, I've been privileged to contribute my expertise to various companies and nonprofits, collaborating with passionate individuals who resonate with my vision.

Navigating this journey hasn't been without its fair share of challenges. Every swell and dip has presented its own set of hurdles to overcome. Yet, through it all, I've found solace and guidance in the wisdom imparted by my father. His life and words have been a steady beacon that lit the path forward during moments of uncertainty and difficulty.

Like Father, Like Daughter

Since childhood, our parents have played an integral role in holistically shaping my siblings and me. They instilled in us the values of perseverance and resilience while nurturing our humanity, providing us with both roots to stay grounded and wings to pursue our life purpose.

While our mother, Carmelita Estrevillo, cultivated our empathy and understanding, it was our father, Josefino "Joe" Estrevillo, who emerged as a beacon in the world of business, laying the groundwork for our journey ahead. His unwavering encouragement and support fueled our confidence, guiding us through trials and triumphs with invaluable insights and guidance. It was under his mentorship that my passion for business flourished, setting me on a path toward entrepreneurial success.

My father's life is my ultimate source of inspiration and influenced the way I do business. His journey was far from easy, marked by a series of unfortunate events that tested his endurance and resilience. Despite the challenges he faced, he emerged highly respected, and known for his integrity and character. Many looked up to him due to the way he lived his life, navigating hardships with grace and determination. Though he's no longer here, I strive to honor his legacy by living up to his example.

Praise God for unlimited opportunities.
Spread your wings and soar higher.

His words of wisdom resonate deep within me. They have influenced my choices and behavior in every aspect of my life. I fondly recall the beginnings of my entrepreneurial journey right after college, when my father and I would regularly gather at our favorite spot in Tomas Morato, Quezon City, in the Philippines.

Entering the café, the alluring scent of freshly brewed Vietnamese coffee mingled with the aroma of warm, just-baked coffee buns. Soft tunes wafted through the cozy atmosphere, setting the stage for our discussions. While my father leisurely pored over the daily paper, I took charge of our customary order, eager to relish our favorite beverages and pastries. With each sip of the robust coffee and every bite of the indulgent bun, I absorbed the wisdom my father imparted, eagerly soaking up his business insights.

Gradually, our discussions veered toward our aspirations. It was in the series of conversations during our regular coffee sessions leading up to his 60th birthday that he condensed his life experiences into four distinct phases, culminating in the creation of a powerful message he called "The Four S's of Joe's Life Story."

1. **SURVIVAL.** In the heart of the city, my father's family of ten endured poverty in a slum community, toiling tirelessly from dawn until dusk. Each day began with a trip to the market to buy and sell vegetables. My father, the eldest son, was attending school in a uniform worn daily. Evenings were spent scavenging for recyclables and crafting makeshift bags from discarded cement. But their lives were upended by a devastating fire that destroyed their tools for their livelihood.

   "Poverty made us easy victims of tragedy and illnesses."

Tragedy struck when my father's younger brother was mistaken for someone else and fatally stabbed, further deepening the family's grief. Financial constraints prevented them from affording proper medical care, leading to his untimely passing. This loss compounded the sorrow of losing Joe's mother at 18 and another sibling months later to the same heart condition. Meanwhile, their father, consumed by grief, emotionally withdrew, diminishing his ability to support the family. Despite these challenges, young Joe took on the role of primary provider, determined to lift them out of poverty.

Their struggles worsened when they were evicted from the slum, and Joe fell ill, requiring hospitalization. He recovered in the countryside with relatives, and one day found himself at the seashore, vowing to work even harder to achieve financial success by the age of 28.

2. **SUCCESS.** After recovering in the countryside, Joe returned to the city with renewed determination, rallying his siblings to *strive harder*. He devised a smart plan to streamline operations in the wet market, convincing stall owners to order through him, which saved them time and money. With bulk orders, Joe secured discounted rates and soon became a wholesaler, a testament to his entrepreneurial spirit.

Education was paramount for Joe, who balanced work and studies to complete a four-year college course in six years. After graduation, he landed a job in the automobile industry, where his commitment and hard work were quickly acknowledged. He earned three promotions in three years and enjoyed perks like a company car. Joe's drive didn't stop there; he also sold insurance to supplement his income, demonstrating his relentless pursuit of success. Marrying my mother, a registered nurse, further solidified his journey toward a prosperous future.

"This is it!"

Joe's achievement marked the realization of his lifelong aspirations. However, a lawsuit within his company led him to question his future as an employee. Determined to chart his own path, he ventured into the modiste and tailor supply business, seeking to meet industry demands. Convincing his wife, a candidate for head nurse, to resign and join him as a business partner solidified his commitment to entrepreneurship.

"Perseverance, honesty, and hard work paid off!"

Joe's business thrived through strategic networking and a steadfast commitment to reliability. It served a diverse clientele, from prominent fashion designers to SMEs and large corporations. They supplied uniforms, set designs, and props for various media productions, among others. This solidified their reputation as a trusted industry supplier and propelled Joe toward the success he had long pursued: rich at the age of 28.

"The world measured success by the things that you own, but I measured success by my ability to acquire the things I was deprived of in the past."

Papa Joe's efforts to secure his family's future were driven by determination and foresight. By acquiring multiple properties, he ensured they would never again fear displacement. Additionally, he fully financed his children's education at the country's top four universities, offering them promising prospects. Comprehensive health and life insurance policies covered every family member, relieving Joe's concerns about their medical needs. Weekly family gatherings, whether at five-star hotels or simple picnics, further strengthened their bond, free from worries about hunger.

With successful businesses and a committed staff, Joe's work-related anxieties disappeared. Owning multiple vehicles allowed us to travel the world comfortably; a stark contrast to past struggles. Ultimately, Joe's financial stability empowered him to provide his family with the security they deserved, fulfilling his lifelong quest for justice.

3. **SATISFACTION.** Satisfaction, defined as the feeling of being fulfilled or contented, drove Joe's pursuit of success. However, despite his achievements, he felt a sense of emptiness, leading him to neglect his family in his relentless quest for wealth. This pursuit ultimately left him isolated and disillusioned, and he realized the elusiveness of peace in his life.

"If you live by satisfying yourself with temporal things, you can never be satisfied."

After years of relentless striving and pursuing success, Joe found himself yearning for something more meaningful. Despite his achievements and accumulation of wealth, he felt a void within him that material possessions could not fill. It dawned on him that true fulfillment lay not in external accomplishments but in making a difference in the lives of others and contributing to something greater than himself.

4. **SIGNIFICANCE.** Joe's pursuit of material success proved hollow, despite his accumulation of wealth, leading him to seek comfort in religious sacrifices, good works, and charitable donations. However, he soon realized that genuine fulfillment couldn't be bought. Wealth only heightened his fears and anxieties, prompting him to change his routines for safety. Amid life's chaos, Joe discovered that true abundance came from a divine source, finding relief as he surrendered his self-sufficiency to his Creator.

This transformation was catalyzed by an outreach event attended by his children, which opened the door for Joe and his wife to embrace the salvific message and embark on a path of spiritual and entrepreneurial fulfillment. Inspired by his newfound faith and sense of purpose, Joe ventured into ministry, becoming a pastor and entrepreneur, seeking to share his spiritual journey and business acumen with others in his community.

Embracing servant leadership, Pastor Joe unearthed the fulfillment and significance he yearned for. Realizing that true wealth lay in his relationships, he reprioritized his life, putting his faith and family over material wealth. It was through this shift in perspective that he finally gained the inner peace he had long sought after. He carved out time to nurture these connections while balancing his commitments to both business and ministry. He treasured his relationship with his Maker, his wife, his children, his family and friends, those divinely entrusted in his care, and others within his sphere of influence, recognizing them as the most precious and priceless wealth.

Enriched by serving the Lover of our souls and embracing a heaven-ward purpose, Pastor Joe's life exemplified genuine richness, success, and accomplishment. Until his final breath, he touched countless lives by sharing the life-changing message of living life to the fullest through the Sacred Way.

My father, Pastor Joe, had a profound understanding of the seasons of life, facing each with unwavering courage and determination. His entrepreneurial success was not just the result of hard work but also his willingness to innovate and adapt to the changing circumstances of each season. He approached every aspect of his career with meticulous attention to detail, utilizing whatever resources were at his disposal to expand and grow. Despite failures he met along the way, he saw them as opportunities to learn and grow, and used them as stepping stones to eventual success. He took full ownership of his journey, defining success on his terms and never compromising his values.

His journey of scaling went beyond business; it was also reflected in his personal life and influenced not only his generation but also those who came after him. The lessons he learned and the courage he displayed in each season became invaluable teachings that he passed down to his children, including myself, and are now principles that I also impart to my son. His legacy is a reminder that success is not just about achieving financial prosperity but also about facing life's challenges head-on, with resilience, integrity, and unwavering determination.

As Numerous as the Stars in the Sky

I feel incredibly fortunate to have grown up in a home with such loving and supportive parents. I was born into the world when my parents were busy nurturing their business startup. Living in a compound of relatives on my grandmother's property meant adhering to communal rules—a lesson in adaptability and cooperation. As we carefully navigated our shared space, my parents, fueled by my father's tenacity and entrepreneurial prowess, were making significant strides in the business world.

I vividly recall the moment when everything changed drastically. As a toddler, I witnessed our transition into our new home, and what a magical place it was! The staircase curved gracefully like those in the fairytales I heard, where princesses seemed to float down them with ease. A magnificent chandelier adorned the ceiling, reminiscent of the ones I admired in fantasy films. Outside, a fountain graced the driveway, inviting me to climb and spend endless hours pretending to be the mermaid I had always dreamt of becoming. The garden became my playground, with lush greenery to frolic amongst, and an authentic nipa hut served as my very own playhouse, igniting my imagination and filling my days with endless adventures.

My childhood was a kaleidoscope of experiences, blending vibrant hues with darker shades. Despite seemingly having everything a modern middle-class family could desire, my siblings and I saw less and less of our parents, who were consumed with creating wealth. As a result, I grappled with trauma after trauma at a tender age, feeling lost in the shadows. However, a beacon of light shattered the darkness when my parents' spiritual journey took a profound turn, leading them to embrace The Way, The Truth, and The Life. With my father's newfound faith anchoring his leadership, material riches took a backseat, and we, his children, became the center of his true inheritance on earth.

As we grew older, my parents immersed us in their entrepreneurial endeavors. We were asked to participate in various aspects of their expanding business empire. By then, they were managing not just one but several enterprises: multiple stalls and covert warehouses in the textile and tailoring industry nationwide, overseeing properties both in metropolitan and provincial areas, operating a purified water business servicing residential neighborhoods and commercial districts, and managing life insurance and employment agencies, among others. This exposure not only provided us with valuable experience but also instilled in us the importance of diligence, innovation, and adaptability in the dynamic world of business.

As I entered my teenage years, around the same age my son is now, my father invested in a small-scale enterprise for my brother and me to co-manage. It was a simple stainless steel food vending cart catering to street food enthusiasts. We were required to maintain its cleanliness, keep it well-stocked, and be ready to serve customers on the go. Little did I know that this venture would teach us invaluable business lessons that have shaped my approach to various endeavors up to this day.

From the daily routines of preparation and financial management to crafting marketing strategies aimed at achieving sell-out success, we gained a wealth of knowledge. Each day provided new insights into inventory management, future planning, and the financial aspects guiding my father's investment. Weekly meetings at my father's office further solidified these lessons, leaving indelible memories that feel as fresh today as they did when they first occurred.

The lessons I learned from my father I aim to instill in my son, Samuel Tupas. I've been intimately involved in every aspect of his upbringing, with a singular goal to "train up [my son] in the [confident, courageous, compassionate] way he should go," so that when my time in his world ends, he will hold fast to these principles with unwavering determination.

From the moment I first heard our son's heartbeat echo through the monitors, I committed myself to being an intentional and purposeful parent who will guide him every step of the way, ensuring that he grows into a confident and independent individual, ready to face the world with fervor and grace.

Reflecting on my journey, I'm immensely proud to witness my 13-year-old son thrive in his entrepreneurial venture. He manages every aspect of his custom-made pin business, serving local businesses in our cozy Northern Arizona town. His entrepreneurial drive isn't new; he's been by my side since infancy, even experiencing his first taste of the world during my work trips, like the one to Sydney, Australia. Inspired by his curiosity, I founded School in a Backpack, focused on equipping the next generation with experiential learning and character education. I'm dedicated to nurturing curious individuals who will challenge norms and forge their own paths, with my son as my inspiration.

Myth-Busting Five Traditional Business Sayings

Within the ever-evolving landscape of entrepreneurship, achieving success often demands a readiness to defy the norm, extend beyond comfort zones, and turn obstacles into opportunities through courage.

Just as life forms on Earth adapt and evolve, entrepreneurs must navigate the dynamic realm of business. While certain principles endure, conventional wisdom invites us to question their validity and chart new courses.

As contemporary business leaders, we grasp the significance of challenging norms, discovering effective leadership approaches for remarkable progress, and laying the groundwork for future generations. In our endeavor to shape the budding minds and bold spirits of tomorrow's business leaders, we delve into the realms of innovation, scaling, and business success.

NEW INSIGHT 1: SWEAT THE SMALL STUFF

The keys to innovation, scaling, and, ultimately, success often lie in the intricate details.

It all starts with a clear understanding of your WHY: What's the driving force behind your endeavor? Keep your sights set on the end goal by pinpointing the problem you're addressing and the unique solutions you bring to the table. Be deliberate and purposeful in your approach: Map out your vision and craft a mission that aligns with your objectives. Break down your goals into manageable steps and take intentional action.

In the ever-evolving landscape of business, it's crucial to stay informed and continuously educate yourself—cultivate a mindset of grit and growth, dedicate time to doing your homework, research industry trends, and stay updated on the latest developments. Foster a passion for lifelong learning, acknowledging the profound impact of knowledge on achievement. Invest in your personal and professional development through various educational avenues such as formal courses, workshops, or independent study. By maintaining a curious and proactive approach to acquiring knowledge, you empower yourself to navigate evolving conditions and capitalize on emerging opportunities.

Success comes from consistently putting in the work, even if it means getting your hands dirty with seemingly trivial tasks. Remember, every successful business journey begins with a small seed of potential, ready to grow into something remarkable.

NEW INSIGHT 2: DO WHAT YOU MUST, FOR WHAT YOU LOVE

Did you know that your talents extend far beyond one area? Your uniqueness lies in the versatility of your skills, cognitive ability, and creativity. With this understanding, you possess the potential for innovation, scaling, and entrepreneurial success.

It must be acknowledged that not everyone pursuing their passions achieves fame or recognition. Our aspirations aren't always in sync with the flow of life. The problem with the often-overused advice of "do what you love" in business is that it confines you to a narrow perspective, limiting your potential. To break free from these constraints, expand your thinking and embrace your multifaceted interests. Start by identifying keywords related to your various passions. Take personality and strengths-finder tests to gain deeper insights about yourself. Craft a compelling narrative that elucidates why you've chosen this business path, harmonizing with your core values and ultimate life goals. Create personas that reflect individuals who share your passions and aspirations. They serve as reflections of the real people you aim to connect with and engage within your community and industry.

While your journey may not align precisely with what you "love," it moves you closer to fulfilling your diverse passions in life. Whether you're driven by projects you're deeply passionate about or motivated by making a positive impact on the lives of those you care about, each step brings you closer to realizing your many "loves." It's about reframing the narrative from "do what you love" to "love what you do," acknowledging and embracing the highlights and positives inherent in your current endeavors.

NEW INSIGHT 3: START WITH WHAT YOU HAVE

Believe it or not, once you have the idea and the passion locked in for your business startup, you've already laid the crucial groundwork.

While having ample funding and top-notch equipment can be advantageous, lacking these shouldn't deter you from getting started. Instead, get creative with your initial resources. It's not always about how much you have; sometimes, it's about leveraging what you already possess and tapping into your network for support. In many cases, it's your connections that will spread the word about your venture, propelling you into the fast lane of the business world.

Additionally, consider your current job as a potential source of funds; keeping your job can provide the financial support needed for your startup until your efforts begin to generate sustainable income. This approach allows you to gradually transition into full-time entrepreneurship while minimizing financial risk and ensuring stability during the early stages of your business. As my husband, Ronald Tupas, says, *"Let your day job cover your expenses while you work on your startup, until your startup gains traction and becomes your primary occupation."*

Remember, in the realm of startups, small actions can yield significant results, taking it slow can lead to rapid progress, and maintaining a steady pace fosters long-term stability.

NEW INSIGHT 4: FAILURE TO LAUNCH CAN BE SUCCESS

Life teeters on the edge between success and failure, each offering invaluable lessons crucial for personal growth and advancement. How can I be so certain of this delicate balance? Simply ask yourself: Do I halt at the pinnacle of success, deeming it my ultimate destination? Similarly, do I surrender at the precipice of failure, viewing it as my final stop? Undoubtedly, the answer to both queries echoes with a firm no.

Embrace failure as a teacher, understanding that its lessons are as valuable as those of success. View obstacles as opportunities for reinvention, each one a step toward achieving your goals. Learn from setbacks to refine your strategies and pivot when necessary. If you find yourself off track, don't give up. Instead, reassess and realign with your true purpose.

The essence of reinvention lies in reconnecting with ourselves. Have we strayed so far from our essence that we no longer recognize ourselves in our pursuits? If so, let's embark on a journey back to our origins, rediscovering the heart and soul of our aspirations. Success, after all, is a subjective journey, and the true measure lies in aligning our achievements with our authentic selves.

NEW INSIGHT 5: SUCCESS IS SUBJECTIVE

Certainly, innovation, scaling, and business success don't come in a one-size-fits-all package.

There's no universal formula for achieving these goals; success varies from person to person. While some may define success by extravagant indulgence, others find it in meeting basic needs. Yet, relying on a single metric for success can feel stifling. Society often imposes its own standards of success, but it's time to break free from those constraints.

Let's dare to chart our own course and redefine success on our terms. Imagine building a community that shares this alternative vision of success. Tailor your business to serve this community, and then scale to reach similar groups. By doing so, you'll not only attain business success but also make a profound impact on the lives of those who resonate with your vision.

Ancient Wisdom

In today's expansive digital realm, amidst the multitude of voices and torrents of information, there exists a wellspring of deep knowledge that has stood the test of time. The ancient scriptures begin with a timeless revelation:

"IN THE BEGINNING, GOD CREATED."

I wholeheartedly believe that the opening phrase of this divinely-inspired text holds the essence—an unhidden secret—to innovation, scaling, and success, be it in business, life, or any aspect thereof.

"In the beginning…"

Everything worthwhile commences at the beginning. Every journey for innovation begins with a single step—the inception of an idea, the spark of creativity, or the decision to challenge the status quo. Whether we stand poised at the starting line, meticulously crafting our business blueprints, or find ourselves picking up the pieces after a stumble, ready to embark on a fresh start, the essence remains the same: All good things start at the beginning. Whether we're charting new territory in unexplored markets, revolutionizing existing industries, or reimagining our approach after setbacks, it all starts at the beginning. So, take that first step.

Every fresh start not only harbors promise but also symbolizes a vital step toward greatness. In the realm of innovation, each commencement carries the potential for transformative change, serving as a crucial element in our quest for progress and success.

"...God..."

Just as the Divine has entrusted us with the responsibility to bear fruit, multiply, and expand, so too are we tasked with scaling our endeavors in the earthly realm. As image-bearers of our Creator, imbued with the divine spark of creativity and innovation, we possess the unique capability to expand our impact and influence.

Like stewards of divine provision, we have the innate ability to grow and extend our efforts, reflecting the divine mandate to co-manage and cultivate the world around us. Just as the divine blueprint guided creation, our vision and efforts are guided by a higher purpose, enabling us to scale our ventures and bring about transformative change in our spheres of influence.

"...created."

Business success is intricately linked to our innate ability to keep creating, pushing the boundaries of what's possible. This creative drive forms the cornerstone of every flourishing enterprise, propelling growth and prosperity. As entrepreneurs, we revel in the process of transforming our visions into reality, undeterred by the passage of time. Waiting time doesn't mean wasted time; rather, it presents an opportunity for reflection, refinement, and further ideation. Our ongoing commitment not only fuels our own success but also catalyzes progress and positive change within our industries and communities.

"I'm back at square one," I muttered, gazing at the myriad of business ideas gathering dust on my shelf. Let's dive into a candid conversation about something we know too well: courage.

Remember those times you poured your heart into a business plan, only to watch it fizzle out? That feeling of trying to keep your head above water in a sea of expectations? And the sting of disappointment when your ideas didn't take off as planned? It's tough, I know.

But in those moments, remember the courage of those who have gone before us and our resilience to adapt to change. Let's remember the wisdom passed down from generations past and internalize those lessons, as we recognize that with every challenge, there's a chance for growth and innovation.

You know what? It's perfectly okay to feel overwhelmed, even unprepared for what's ahead. It's all part of the journey.

Trust me, I've been in those shoes more times than I can count.

Gemma Bulos

Founder & CEO of The Reinventor Lab LLC

https://www.linkedin.com/in/gemmabulos
https://www.facebook.com/gemmabulos
https://www.instagram.com/gemmabulos
https://www.gemmabulos.com
https://www.reinventorlab.com

Gemma draws on her vast experience as a multi-award-winning social entrepreneur, global speaker, educator, musician, movement builder, and filmmaker to catalyze change in the world. Recognized globally for her expertise in imposter syndrome and designing for social impact, she supports purpose-driven start-up founders, coaches, and business owners to improve the world AND make money. Gemma won Best Social Entrepreneur in Asia award from the World Economic Forum; has delivered hundreds of talks in 36 countries (including 3 TEDx) alongside Nobel Peace Laureates and world leaders; and taught Social Entrepreneurship at Stanford University. Despite her extraordinary achievements, Gemma grappled with imposter syndrome throughout her life, driving her to develop tools for overcoming it. Today, she coaches emerging change agents worldwide, empowering them to amplify their impact and visibility by establishing thought leadership and adopting agile, sustainable business practices. Visit gemmabulos.com to explore how Gemma can help future-proof your business and career.

IMPOSTER TO I'MPOWERED: UNLEASHING YOUR POWER WITHIN TO LIVE A LIFE OF PURPOSE

By Gemma Bulos

In 2001, I was living what I thought was my biggest dream—working as a professional jazz singer in the heart of New York City. Picture it: Me, crooning on stage with world-famous musicians like Les Paul, rubbing elbows with my celebrity idols like Roberta Flack and Nile Rodgers, and waiting for that big break I knew in my bones was right around the corner. It was a dream that had taken root way back at my fourth-grade talent show when I sang Karen Carpenter's "For All We Know," and wow, did it feel like magic! I was hooked—I just knew I belonged onstage.

But fate had its own plans, which didn't play out exactly the way I had imagined in my dreams.

Fast forward to that fateful Tuesday in September 2001. I was supposed to be in the World Trade Center when the plane struck the first building. But by some twist of fate, I called in sick that day. It rocked me to my core and made me question everything about my life. Why am I here? Why wasn't I there? What do I do now? I realized that my life as I knew it was over. Being the new Ella Fitzgerald or winning five Grammys suddenly didn't matter anymore.

In the midst of this existential crisis, I realized that gratitude and purpose would be my guiding lights. I knew I had to find ways to make a difference in the world, to live a life of deep service with unwavering purpose.

And so began a rollercoaster ride of reinvention that has defined the past two decades of my life. From jazz singer to grassroots peace activist to humanitarian to changemaker—in each new chapter I found that the deeper I immersed myself in my purpose, the greater the impact exceeded my wildest dreams. But amidst the triumphs and accolades, there lurked a familiar adversary that challenged me at every corner: imposter syndrome.

Yep, that pesky little voice of doubt was a constant companion—especially in times of transition when I was diving into the unknown. It whispered insidiously, planting seeds of uncertainty and questioning my abilities at every turn. But here's the kicker: with every reinvention, I not only faced imposter syndrome head-on but found a way to emerge stronger, more capable, more competent, and, most importantly, more impactful. It's been a journey marked not by the absence of self-doubt, but by the triumph over it—a journey that led me to uncover three powerful approaches to navigating the rough seas of uncertainty and come out more confident and I'mPowered.

No, that's not a typo. Let's talk about this concept I've come to embrace: I'mPower. While "empower" implies a transfer of power from one entity to another, I'mPower transcends this paradigm. I'mPower isn't about waiting for someone else to give you power. It's about recognizing the power that already exists within you. It's not a verb or a noun—In my mind, it's a truth. It's about tapping into your innate strength, experience, and passion to effect change in the world around you.

So, armed with the understanding that I'mPower is not just a concept but a reality, let's dive into three pivotal moments where I faced imposter syndrome head-on and emerged I'mPowered. These are the moments that shaped me, challenged me, and ultimately propelled me forward on my journey of self-discovery and growth.

Building a Global Peace Movement: There Is No "Me" in "Choir!"

In the aftermath of September 11th, 2001, the world felt like it had shifted on its axis. Walking the streets of New York City in those somber days, I witnessed something extraordinary—a profound shift in the way people connected with one another. Suddenly, amidst the grief and sorrow, strangers acknowledged each other's presence, shared a collective understanding of loss and resilience, and helped one another in deep and profound ways.

It was during this tumultuous time that I felt compelled to find a source of inspiration—a beacon of hope to guide not only my own healing but also that of others. And so, I turned to music, composing a song called "We Rise" as a tribute to the human spirit's capacity to overcome adversity and unite in solidarity.

But my vision didn't stop there. Inspired by the newfound sense of connection and community exhibited by New Yorkers in response to 9/11, I embarked on a mission to bring people together, this time not through grief but through our shared dreams for ourselves and our families—opportunity, health, wealth, peace. So, I left my life, career, and relationship, gave away my belongings, and let go of my rent-controlled NYC apartment, which proves I was serious! With little more than a backpack, a guitar, and a few hundred dollars in my bank account, I set out to build what I affectionately dubbed the "Million Voice Choir"—a movement aimed at spreading a message of peace and unity through song.

As I traveled the world, extending invitations to individuals to join this global peace movement, I encountered countless acts of generosity and kindness. From strangers offering transportation to conferences and concerts to individuals providing shelter and support along the way, to benefactors handing me thousands of dollars to continue my journey, I was overwhelmed by the outpouring of support for the cause.

But amidst the excitement and momentum of the Million Voice Choir, doubts began to creep in. Who was I to spearhead such a monumental endeavor? Did I have what it takes to bring people together on such a grand scale? Who did I think I was? Gem-Madonna? The familiar whispers of imposter syndrome threatened to derail my efforts at every turn.

However, as I immersed myself in the project, I realized that the Million Voice Choir was not about me—it was about something much bigger. It was about harnessing the collective power of individuals worldwide to affect positive change. In embracing this truth, I shifted my perspective, recognizing that my role was not to be the sole driving force behind the movement but rather a conduit for the voices of millions to be heard.

And so, armed with a newfound sense of purpose and determination, I pressed forward, overcoming the doubts and insecurities that once plagued me. The Million Voice Choir became a symbol of unity and a testament to the resilience of the human spirit in the face of adversity.

On September 21, 2004, after crisscrossing the globe non-stop, tirelessly teaching people the song and rallying communities to join our cause, the moment we had all been waiting for finally arrived. From the bustling streets of New York City to the remote corners of the world, choirs in over 100 cities across 60 countries joined together in harmony, raising their voices to sing "We Rise." It was an awe-inspiring display of unity, a testament to the power of music to transcend borders and bring people together in pursuit of a common goal.

Through this movement, I learned that imposter syndrome thrives on the belief that our worthiness and abilities are inherently tied to our individual identities. By reframing my perspective and recognizing the collective nature of the Million Voice Choir, I was able to overcome imposter syndrome and embrace the power of community, not my ego, in driving positive change.

A Single Drop Starts a Wave: Embracing the Unknown

While I was busy building the Million Voice Choir and spreading the message of "We Rise," I often used a phrase I coined to invite others to join our cause: "It takes a single drop of water to start a wave." This simple metaphor became a rallying cry, encouraging people to recognize the power of their actions to create ripples of change—that their every thought, word, and action was that drop and would affect everything around them.

As I traveled the globe, sharing the song and its message, invitations poured in from conferences worldwide, covering topics ranging from environmental justice to conflict resolution to peace to youth empowerment to interfaith initiatives, and the list goes on. It seemed that everywhere I turned, people were eager to support our mission.

All of these conferences made sense as they aligned with peace. But there was one invitation that came out of nowhere. In 2003, I received an unexpected invitation to the Water for Life conference at the United Nations. Apparently, because of my "single drop" metaphor, I had become known as the "water lady," the lady singing for water. Little did I know, this gathering would alter the course of my life's journey. Here I was, this singer with this hippy-dippy message that we're all drops of water and have the ability to change the world, blah blah blah, presenting alongside researchers, experts, and leaders who were all trying to solve the global water crisis! It was there, amidst these discussions, that I had a profound realization: The metaphorical significance of water in my song had a tangible counterpart in the real world.

Learning about the staggering statistics—one out of seven people lack access to fresh water, children die every 15 seconds from dirty water, half the hospital beds are occupied by people with water-related diseases—was a game changer. Learning that women and girls collectively spend billions of hours a day fetching water, which means they can't work or go to school, flipped my life upside down. Suddenly, my song was no longer just a metaphor; it became my cause, my destiny.

As the world came together to sing "We Rise," I couldn't shake the bittersweet realization that peace—*true* peace—required more than just unity of voices. It required action, and my action was clear: bring clean water to those in need.

After mobilizing the choir, determined to make a difference, I immersed myself in the study of the water crisis, uncovering stories of grassroots movements fighting for their rights to clean water. In my global travels, I witnessed firsthand how women and girls were disproportionately affected by the lack of water and sanitation and how communities cannot escape the cycle of poverty because not having access to this vital resource affects health, food security, education, energy, productivity, income, and the local economy. Inspired by their resilience, I set out to learn simple yet effective ways to bring clean water and sanitation to communities worldwide.

My journey led me to the Philippines, a nation ravaged by record numbers of natural disasters every year and lacking vital infrastructure to effectively manage clean water resources for every citizen. Here, I saw the urgent need for sustainable solutions in my country of heritage.

After conducting extensive research, I learned to build a simple water treatment technology that could be manufactured anywhere in the world using basic materials like cement, sand, and gravel. This innovation had never been introduced to the Philippines before, offering a promising solution to their water crisis.

The moment I stepped foot in the Philippines, I was buzzing with misguided confidence, ready to change the world with the skills honed from my choir-building days. Without a second thought, I reached out to the big guns: the head of UNICEF, Oxfam, Plan International, and even the Ambassador to Canada, pitching partnerships with a fire in my heart. Driven by a mission to bring clean water and sanitation to communities, I felt unstoppable. The cause was monumental, greater than myself, fuelling my courage to connect with the seemingly unreachable.

To my surprise, these giants listened. Shared visions have power, and despite being a newcomer without a track record, I managed to secure partnerships with all three international aid organizations and was granted a whopping $50,000 from the Canadian Ambassador. The icing on the cake? Another $10,000 award from Queen Latifah and Covergirl for Women Changing the World Through Music, providing more seed money to launch our initiatives.

With funds and partnerships in hand, it was go-time. Time to suit up, get my hands dirty, and do what I promised! My excitement was soon shattered when I realized that I now had to execute, plunging me into a whirlwind of unfamiliar challenges and overwhelming fears. The imposter syndrome that I thought I had left behind came crashing back with a vengeance. Here I was, stepping onto a path vastly different from building the choir where my musical background and wanderlust had once bolstered my confidence. Suddenly, I was a stranger in a land of construction, engineering, and international development, fields in which I had no footing. The internal cacophony of doubt was deafening, each voice a sharp question mark against my abilities, my potential impact, and the terrifying possibility of inadvertently causing harm. The voices kept saying, "I don't know what I'm doing!" And they were right! I didn't! The stories I had heard of well-intentioned people and organizations failing despite abundant resources, experience, and expertise haunted me, echoing my deepest fears. Could I really fulfill my promises? And would it have the impact I projected?

In this unfamiliar terrain, I discovered the power of learned optimism. The concept of "learned optimism," a term coined by Dr. Martin Seligman, a pioneer in the field of positive psychology, serves as a contrast to "learned helplessness." This narrative flip shines a light on the stark difference between succumbing to the belief that we are powerless in the face of adversity and recognizing that, while we may not control every aspect of our circumstances, we hold the power to choose our response. In embodying this philosophy, we do not merely skirt around life's difficulties but engage with them in a way that promotes growth, courage, and an unshakeable belief in our ability to prevail. As a tool, it teaches us to catch and change our negative thoughts, flipping them into positive ones. It's like learning to see the glass half full instead of half empty, helping us to move past our doubts and fears. By practicing optimism, we start to view challenges not as roadblocks but as opportunities to grow stronger and more capable. It's not about ignoring life's struggles; it's about facing them with a heart full of hope and a mind focused on solutions. This approach isn't just a feel-good theory—it's a practical way to live life, lighting our way through tough times and leading us toward our dreams and goals.

For me, this wasn't about plastering a smile over my fears or denying the weight of the challenge ahead. It was about retraining my mind to focus on solutions rather than getting entangled in debilitating fears. My mantra became, "I don't know what I'm doing, YET. But I will learn. Just like I learned to walk, read, write, and build a global peace movement."

This shift in mindset, acknowledging my current lack of knowledge as a temporary state, opened the door to growth and learning. It was about embracing the journey of acquiring new skills, not dwelling on current limitations. Each setback became a lesson, enlightening me on the resilience required to push forward. I learned that optimism is a skill honed through perseverance and the relentless belief in our capacity to make a difference. This mindset transformed my approach, turning despair into determination and doubt into dedication. It has powered me to see beyond the immediate hurdles and envision the thriving communities that our projects would support. Optimism and curiosity, I realized, are the most powerful tools in a changemaker's arsenal, fueling the drive to learn and listen deeply so we can uplift lives and reshape futures.

In the initial three months, we trained communities across the Philippines to build simple water filters, ensuring they had clean water for a lifetime. As a standalone project, it was a failure. We soon realized technology alone wasn't the answer. The real challenge lay in the project's sustainability after we left. The communities lacked the necessary resources, finances, and community buy-in to ensure the sustainability of the project. Once they left the training, it was highly unlikely that the project would ever get off the ground.

That's when we pivoted. We began to engage with the communities, listening to their stories, hopes, dreams, and ideas, and we discovered their profound desire for self-sufficiency. They didn't want handouts; they wanted to develop solutions themselves and reinvest in their community's development. Moving away from imposing our solutions, we shifted our approach to one of collaboration, working alongside each community to help them identify their unique challenges and, together, craft a pathway forward. This wasn't about providing solutions but facilitating a process where communities could harness their own resources and creativity to build sustainable futures. This approach fostered community ownership and drew awards and recognition from the World Economic Forum, USAID, Clinton Global Initiative University, and others, validating our community-driven model.

Despite the shadows cast by imposter syndrome, our journey underscored the power of listening, learning, and co-creating with communities. By embracing uncertainty as an opportunity for growth, we sought inspiration from the collective wisdom and resilience of the communities we served. What unfolded was a testament to innovation from genuinely listening to, empathizing with, and up-powering communities—a model that proved effective and deeply transformative. Take that, imposter syndrome!

African Women Water Champions: Creating a New Normal

Following the success of our water work in the Philippines, my path took an inspiring turn toward Sub-Saharan Africa, where I had the honor of partnering with one of my idols—Professor Wangari Maathai. She was not only the first African woman to win the Nobel Peace Prize but also a trailblazer in recognizing the integral link between peace and the environment. Professor Maathai was iconic, fierce, and deeply committed to environmental conservation and women's rights. Being in her orbit and guided by her wisdom to bring our community-driven model to Africa, with a primary focus on upskilling grassroots women, was a moment of profound personal and professional significance for me. The stories of transformation I witnessed there, of women leading their communities in tree planting, water conservation, and sustainable agriculture, were not just inspiring but deeply affirming. It validated our work in the Philippines and reinforced my belief that when communities are given the tools to shape their own destiny, they can and will flourish beyond imagination. This chapter in Africa, guided by the spirit and wisdom of Professor Maathai, remains one of the most life-changing periods in my journey, illustrating the profound impact of building women's leadership in environmental sustainability.

In Sub-Saharan Africa and across the globe, the task of water gathering and all water-related chores falls squarely on the shoulders of women and girls. They can spend upwards of eight hours per day taking daily treks over rough terrains, carrying over 42 pounds of water along with laundry, children, dirty dishes, and pots. They fetch water from unprotected sources that are shared by animals and full of contaminants, risking their health and safety. Perhaps unsurprisingly, this strenuous and dangerous responsibility leads to low- to no-income-generating productivity for women, increased school dropout rates among girls, and amplifies the vulnerabilities to attacks during these daily treks for both.

Diving into Sub-Saharan Africa, I found myself in a sea of uncertainty and self-doubt, a very different experience from the familiar comforts of the Philippines. Back home, my heritage and understanding wove seamlessly into the cultural tapestry. There, gender roles, often less rigid, allowed women to ascend to leadership with relative ease—exhibited by the election of two female presidents and the widespread embrace of women in pivotal roles. By stark contrast, Sub-Saharan Africa unfolded a different story, where cultural norms tightly scripted women's roles, erecting barriers that went beyond the social and economic, perpetuating the cycle of poverty from generation to generation.

The challenge, then, was not merely an internal battle adapting to unfamiliar territories or customs but confronting a pervasive imposter syndrome—not just my own, but one rooted in generations of societal conditioning limiting women's roles. The realization dawned on me that imposter syndrome, a term typically reserved for individual experiences of self-doubt, had an external counterpart emerging from traditional beliefs and societal norms that rigidly defined gender roles. It struck me profoundly that the feelings of inadequacy weren't solely internal battles but were arguably born from and perpetuated by external, deeply ingrained cultural narratives.

Facing these profound challenges, our mission transformed, becoming a crusade not merely to challenge but to fundamentally reinvent the ingrained status quo. We embarked on a dedicated program to train women not just as providers of water and sanitation but as pioneers, equipping them with the knowledge and tools to construct sustainable water and sanitation technologies never before accessible in their communities. This upskilling didn't stop with mere training; we instilled in them the skills to become educators themselves, amplifying their impact by teaching others and exponentially increasing their income by professionalizing their services. This process helped them to recognize and quantify the immense value they were adding to their communities.

These brave women took monumental risks, engaging in activities once deemed unthinkable for them, such as climbing ladders, defying deeply rooted prohibitions and venturing into domains traditionally reserved for men. They faced potential ostracization from their communities, humiliation brought upon their families, and harsh criticism from their spouses. Yet, they persevered, driven by an unwavering belief in the transformative power of their work—not just for their immediate families but for their entire communities.

A profound transformation unfolded, one that rewrites the narrative surrounding imposter syndrome. It's a revelation that this crippling self-doubt is sewn into the fabric of societal and cultural beliefs that whisper, sometimes shout, that we're not enough, that we don't belong, or that certain roles are beyond our reach. Training women to construct clean water and sanitation technologies wasn't merely about transferring skills; it was about dismantling centuries-old barriers. With every brick laid, every water tank built, these formidable women chose to rewrite the script. They weren't just challenging cultural norms; they were forging a new vision of what could be—of what was rightfully theirs. These acts of defiance became their breakthroughs, their ladder out of the cycle of poverty and into roles of leadership and innovation. Through their actions, they did not merely envision a new normal—

they built it, brick by brick, demonstrating that change, though fraught with challenges, was within grasp. And in this transformation, they offered not just hope but tangible proof that the chains of tradition could be broken, paving the way for a future where their daughters, and the generations to follow, would be bound not by societal limitations but by the breadth of their dreams and the strength of their will.

We saw the tangible, measurable impact of their work in the stories that emerged from local clinics and schools, where our trainees' projects significantly improved access to essential services. One such clinic, previously reliant on distant water sources, could now provide continuous care and expand its services, all thanks to the infrastructure built by the women we trained. Such achievements improved health outcomes and elevated the clinic's status, showcasing the profound effects of uplifting women to challenge and change their realities.

In a game-changing move, schools transformed from places for book learning to hubs of hope and action, thanks to the leadership of our remarkable women. They began by building their first projects on school grounds, realizing how important their children's education was for breaking the cycle of poverty. However, this move did something even more remarkable; it broke the cycle that kept girls out of school, especially due to activities like fetching water or missing school because they got their periods. With access to water and proper toilets at their schools, girls were able to stay in class, learn, and grow.

But beyond the tangible benefits of improved access and attendance, the symbolism of women leading these initiatives across schools was electrifying. Witnessing women who looked like their mothers and their grandmothers take charge and solve community problems inspired them. It reshaped perceptions universally—girls and boys alike witnessed first-hand that women, when given the chance, not only thrived in roles traditionally not theirs, but excelled. This visibility was pivotal. Women building, training, and leading projects that improved the community was no longer unusual or surprising; it was *normal.*

The many stories of these incredible women underscore the reality that the battle against imposter syndrome is fought on both internal and external fronts. It's a reminder that when we change the narrative and refuse to be limited by the societal and cultural scripts written for us, we step into our power. We start to see ourselves not as imposters but as pioneers, trailblazers who dare to believe that we are indeed enough and who have the evidence to prove it, time and again, for our families, our communities, and the future we dare to imagine.

Rewriting the Narrative

I've had my fair share of moments when I could've gone down a darker path, all thanks to the self-doubt whispering away inside me. In sharing my battle with imposter syndrome, I've opened up about times I felt unsure, had big realizations, and how I kept pushing through. That determination is what helped me to start fresh, to use my own spark to make the difference I wanted in the world.

Earlier in the chapter, I introduced learned optimism. This technique asks us to confront our inner critic—that quiet yet persistent voice that whispers of inadequacy, doubt, and fear of exposure.

"I'm not enough," it says. "I don't know what I'm doing. I don't belong. Someone will find out I'm a fraud." These statements, dark clouds in our mental sky, often go unchallenged, accepted as truths. Yet, learned optimism challenges us to hold these thoughts to the light, scrutinizing them and asking if they are truthful or permanent.

More often than not, we find that the answer to one or both of these questions is a resolute 'no.' This realization is our turning point. It's the moment when we have the opportunity to reframe our narrative.

When building the choir, it was easy to believe that the weight of the mission rested solely on my shoulders, that somehow, my worth was entangled with its success or failure. I found liberation in understanding that my role was to serve the mission, not to become it. This detachment didn't diminish my contribution, but rather, magnified the importance of the collective over the individual ego.

When launching the water projects in the Philippines, I confronted the permanence of my perceived inadequacies. I challenged myself to see beyond the present moment, recognizing that my lack of knowledge or experience is but a temporary state. Through the practice of learned optimism, I discovered the power of reframing my narrative, transforming negative beliefs into sources of strength and motivation. This shift in perspective is not just about positive thinking; it's about recognizing our capacity for growth and change.

And finally, while training women in Sub-Saharan Africa to be water experts, I took a deeper dive into the systemic roots of imposter syndrome, acknowledging the societal, cultural, and systemic conditions that feed our doubts and sense of inadequacy. Understanding that these feelings are not solely a product of our minds but are also influenced by, if not born of, external societal, familial, cultural, and systemic factors challenges us to change not just our perceptions but the environments that give rise to them.

As we conclude this chapter, I invite you, dear reader, to practice learned optimism by reframing one negative thought each day. Here's how you can commit to starting to rewrite your narrative:

1. **Identify a Negative Thought**: Catch yourself in the moment of doubt or negativity.

2. **Analyze the Thought**: Dissect the thought. Is there evidence to prove that it is truthful or permanent?

3. **Reframe the Thought**: If you can't find evidence of truth or permanence, then you can transform the negative into a positive, actionable statement that propels you forward.

Here's an example of how I used the learned optimism tool when I launched my water projects in the Philippines.

The following is a step-by-step guide that can help you turn negative statements into I'mPowering ones. By following this structured approach, you can transform challenges into opportunities for growth and impact:

Step 1: Identify a Negative Statement. Start by identifying a negative statement that you have been telling yourself. For example,

"I don't know what I'm doing!"

Step 2: Question the Truth and Permanence. Once you have identified your negative statement, ask yourself if the statement is true and if it will be true forever. In the example, the statement

"I don't know what I'm doing!" is true, but it is not necessarily permanent.

Step 3: Reframe with an I'm-Powered Statement. Reframe your negative statement into an I'mPowering one.

For example, *"I may not know what I'm doing YET. But I can learn..."*

Step 4: Make it Affirmational. Enhance your statement with evidence of past achievements.

For example, add *"...just like I've learned how to walk, read, write, and build a global peace movement. I've done harder things."*

Step 5: Outline Productive Action. Specify the actions you can take to achieve your goal.

For example, *"I can do research, find an organization doing great work and learn from them, find a partner who has worked in the water sector in the Philippines, I can learn how to build simple technologies, and most importantly, I can listen to the community and ask them what they want."*

Step 6: Set an Aspirational Goal. Conclude with an aspirational goal that you want to achieve.

For example, *"And as a result, we will design an effective program that provides clean water and sanitation for communities in the Philippines."*

By following these steps, you can apply learned optimism in your life, which can help you turn negative statements into I'mPowering ones. With this approach, you can transform challenges into opportunities for growth and impact.

This practice is not just about combating imposter syndrome; it's a commitment to a lifelong journey of self-discovery, growth, and purposeful living.

From Ripple to Wave

In the closing lines of this chapter, and as a fitting echo to the essence of *Dare to Dream Big*, I find myself contemplating the profound truth that dreaming big is not a singular event but a continuous, unfolding journey. Each time I dared to step beyond the shadows of impostor syndrome, my capacity to dream expanded, inviting even larger visions into reality. Had I allowed the haunting grip of doubt to tether my spirit, the achievements of which I am the most proud might not only have been impossible, they would have been unimaginable. It was not merely about conquering impostor syndrome once but engaging in a relentless dialogue with it, learning to quiet its persistent murmur with the louder, more vibrant voice of my dreams. Had I let my imposter syndrome take the wheel, perhaps I would not have mobilized an unprecedented global peace movement, or given hundreds of talks on stages like the United Nations, speaking alongside Nobel Peace Laureates and global leaders, or taught at Stanford University without a college degree (you can catch that story in my next book, *Sassy, Classy, and Badassy*), or brought clean water to millions of people in Asia and Africa. Any one of those accomplishments alone would have been an audacious dream come true. But each one built on the other, daring me to dream bigger and bolder at every milestone.

This story, my story, underscores a fluidity in dreaming, an encouragement to understand that our dreams and aspirations need not be static but can grow, evolve, and multiply as we do. We are indeed powerful beyond measure, and our dreams, no matter how grand, are valid and attainable. We can redefine our experiences not as limitations, but as stepping stones to a greater destiny and a pathway to bigger dreams. When we choose to view our challenges through the lens of opportunity, every setback becomes a setup for a comeback, every failure a lesson in resilience. This shift in perspective isn't just about positive thinking; it's about actively rewriting our internal dialogue, affirming that we are the architects of our fate, capable of constructing a reality brimming with possibility and promise. It's through daring to dream big, again and again, that we truly realize our potential, breaking barriers and setting new frontiers for ourselves and others.

And so, my friend, are you ready to see what magic unfolds when we pivot our thoughts, shake off our doubts, and truly step into our power? Here's the thing—each time we triumph over a fear or a bout of imposter syndrome, we're not just moving; no, we're soaring toward becoming the most I'mPowered versions of ourselves. And guess what? This is just the start. We're on the brink of something new, a chapter ripe with hurdles, yes, but oh, the discoveries and growth it promises!

Now, I know imposter syndrome likes to sneak up on us, whispering those sneaky doubts. But here's a wild idea: What if we use those whispers as fuel? What if we turn them into a roaring engine pushing us toward the change we crave, in us and around us? The horizon? It's vast and endless, and it's ours for the taking—urging us to keep pushing, keep questioning, and keep leaving our unique stamp on this world.

Let's tackle those negative whispers and toxic stories head-on. It's like flipping the switch in a dark room. By ditching those limiting beliefs and crafting I'mPowering narratives, we unlock boundless possibilities. These aren't just stories; they're pathways illuminated by our dreams, leading us to our grandest ambitions.

There's an entire universe out there, just waiting for us to make our move, to challenge what's given, and to scribble outside the lines. You, my friend, are that single drop—the one that has the potential to start a wave of transformation. Ready to dive into your life of infinite possibilities? Dare to dream big, again and again!

Klara M Reid

Klara Reid
Researcher/Chronic Cellular Dehydration

https://www.facebook.com/KlaraReidGeller?mibextid=ZbWKwL
www.lifeandpassionredefined.com

Born in Transylvania, Romania – December 17th, 1954

Mother tongue: Hungarian

College Diploma in Mechanical Design- Brasov, Romania

Worked as a graphic designer for 8 years.

Got married at age 24, 2 kids

I Immigrated legally to Israel in 1985, from a fully-blown communist dictatorship.

Immigrated legally to Canada in 1987

I lost both my parents soon after I left my home country.

I got out of a bad marriage after 12 years, only one year after we arrived in Canada.

A single mom, for 17 years.

I worked at CIBC for 5 years, starting in 1989.

I got ill, and couldn't work for 1 year.

Became an Independent Insurance broker in 1994, and did it for 22 years

Moved to the West Coast of Canada in 2001.

2011 Got married to Wilfred Reid

In 2012 I started to drink ERW, and my body accepted it.

I started to recover, I read books and literature on dehydration, health etc.

I got better and better and in 2014 finally, I realized that the root cause of my health issues

I had it was nothing else but dehydration.

Since 2014 volunteered with the American Anti-Cancer Institute. www.AmericanACI.org

I retired from the insurance business at the age of 60

8 years of research, and 2 years to write my book in English, which is my 3rd language.

2019- 'The Purple Wave' published – a true story

MICRO-NISHE: Involuntary Chronic Cellular Dehydration and Electrolyzed Reduced Water

Not many know that I am a self-taught 'medical spy', for pharmaceutical scams and health care fraud.

My goal is to participate in this global effort to change this antiquated and manipulative medical system which finally got to a dead end.

It was a tremendous achievement to get my health under control. A down payment on a house was previously spent on my health.

In 2014 we lost our home because I could not work due to autoimmune issues. It is an honour for me to spread the word about this therapeutic tool, which helped me control my health and manage my life beyond belief.

My physical health improved as much as my mental health, ever since I started hydrating with this water. Water, however, is not the only thing I had to do, but it constituted the basis for the change I experienced and without it, it could never have happened.

When I discovered that 90% of the population is dehydrated, I realized that I could help an endless number of people. I dropped everything and I became a world ambassador for this cause. I enjoy helping people and sharing my knowledge. Hobbies: Writing, nature, Biomimicry, interior design, pickleball, table tennis.

THE POSTER CHILD

By Klara M Reid

"When you have something to say, silence is a lie."
—Dr. Jordan Peterson

Not saying anything about this subject, which I am extremely familiar with, does feel like lying, so forgive me for shouting my message to humanity:

LACK OF FUNCTIONAL WATER IS RUINING LIVES BY CAUSING CHRONIC DEHYDRATION ON A CELLULAR LEVEL

How many lives? 7.2 billion, which is roughly 90% of the population! Yes, 90% of people are chronically dehydrated! Hopefully now I have your attention.

A study published in *The New York Post* on January 2nd, 2023 says: *"Not consuming enough water increases the risk of death by twenty percent!"* I respectfully disagree, as I honestly think the percentage is higher, but that isn't important…What is important, and what no one is talking about, is why water, which is the main fuel for humans, is not functional anymore, and what we can do about it!

People are going through life experiencing pain or health problems caused by different stressors or trauma without ever discovering the root cause of the issue. The common belief is that "stress kills." I say that it is dehydration that ultimately kills people when stress happens! I will also present "the solution," because someone has to do it; you will see that most of these tragedies don't have to happen…

Growing up in the '60s, I made the giant mistake of ignoring water for decades. Therefore, I consider myself the forerunner, the messenger if you will, for a condition eloquently called "dehydration" today. I hope this chronicle will simplify things by showing you how to restore physical and mental health, vitality, and spirit with a natural instrument which is crucial because it will reactivate the healing force within. Sadly the majority of people are ignoring this force, so, please keep an open mind.

* * * *

My story starts in 1966 in Eastern Europe. I was a healthy, active child until then, thanks to great, loving parents. I grew up with good nutrition, in a healthy environment with lots of fresh air and exercise. At age twelve, I suddenly became ill due to a hepatitis virus type A, from contaminated tap water in Bucharest. I never completely recovered from this inflammation of the liver; to make things worse, my body no longer accepted tap water. I did not trust water, so I stopped drinking it. When thirsty, I drank a small glass of carbon dioxide-induced mineral water. This turned my life upside down. At the time no one, including myself, was aware of what I was doing, and soon after, weird things started happening to me; I did not do well in stressful situations. Any stress, like an exam at school or in college, or an accident in the family, immediately triggered such turmoil in my life that I needed medical attention. Each time I had a different "diagnosis," as my symptoms were quite different. From panic-like attacks, shortness of breath, acute psychosis, a sense of impending doom, false appendicitis pain, angina pectoris, cavities, and root canals to terrible morning sickness and giving birth prematurely to my daughter and her suffering a stroke at birth, bad stuff was happening to me and these were the labels. Later gallstones, fibroid tumors, and other scary conditions kept interfering with the normal rhythm of my young life. This required constant visits to doctors and specialists, thirteen hospitalizations, and numerous dental appointments. Lots of precious time was wasted, and more importantly, they caused such limitations in my physical and mental activity that I could not live up to my full potential. My condition, rooted in prolonged dehydration, followed me to Israel, and then to Canada.

We left Romania in 1985, leaving behind the communist dictatorship, but the visits to doctors and dentists kept happening. I had surgery after surgery during the nine months when both my parents passed away and I never saw my father after we left—the worst stress of my life! By the time I turned thirty-one, my immune system was seriously compromised and then a cheap dentist in Toronto almost killed me: After a few years, the metals he recklessly used in the amalgams kept leaching into my system. I lived for years with numerous annoying symptoms including candida and extremely achy psoriasis, until the root cause, serious heavy metal poisoning, was discovered by a naturopath. I spent over $50,000 on chelation and treatments to clean mercury, lead, and aluminum out of my system so I could function again. This took another two years of my life. Being dehydrated made it much worse than it had to be. I ended up with a permanent heart condition, called "left anterior hemiblock." I fought a serious fight to stay alive while raising my kids as a single mom, which included lots of research and experiments with diets, healers, and different natural treatments after rejecting doctors who had no answers for me.

Fast forward to 2012…at age 57 I was struggling with low energy, systemic candidiasis, occasional knee pain, atrocious pain from shingles and constant hip discomfort, overall stiffness in my body, terrible muscle spasms, frightful gout, and some auto-immune issues. Crazy, accelerated aging drew a new wrinkle on my face daily, until I was afraid to look into the mirror. I was "diagnosed" with asthma, allergies, arthritis, and sleep apnea. I suffered from chronic fatigue and periodically repeated urinary tract/bladder infections. I was forgetting things and had some anxiety because of this situation. My kids were worried sick. On a Labour Day weekend, we hiked Mount Cheam in Chilliwack, BC, and I couldn't come downhill. It felt like my hips were "bone on bone," which they probably were. Sitting and driving were just impossible for me. I hated the fact that I couldn't function the way I wanted to.

Fred and I had just gotten married, and when we met he was on multiple heart medications. He was addicted to sodas for many years before I met him, which of course caused severe dehydration and acidosis. During the elevated stress he endured due to five deaths in the family (one being his wife) in only two years, he suffered a heart attack and became the victim of a condition called Bell's Palsy. Miraculously he survived, and he recovered well, but ended up with two stents in his arteries.

My daughter, thirty-three at the time, living 6,000 kilometres away, became addicted to Diet Coke. As a direct consequence, she had terrible mood swings and became obese. This caused a spiritual wound for me that I had never experienced before. My very ordinary life was heading in the wrong direction. I couldn't drive and earn enough money, and therefore we struggled with mortgage payments and other expenses. It seemed that I was losing at every front, but I kept my faith, praying cluelessly for a miracle.

* * * *

"If there is magic on this planet, it's contained in water."
—Loren Eiseley

One rainy day in the spring of 2012, Fred came home with a gallon of water received from someone he just met at a meeting. I thought accepting water from a stranger was quite silly and unnecessary but when I tried it, solely out of courtesy, it had a great, clean taste, better than our well water…it was light and refreshing, and strangely enough, my body instantly accepted it. They told us that we could have more, so we kept getting more of this water we did not know anything about. In a few days, my sleep got better and I could digest food without taking multiple enzymes. I enjoyed drinking it and my energy level went nuts. I liked how I felt and I was amazed that the cyst I'd had under my right arm ever since I was breastfeeding my kids suddenly disappeared.

I wanted to learn more, so we went to an info session which turned out to be the best decision of our lives. Everything we saw and heard not only made sense but was quite shocking. It was simple stuff that every soul should be aware of, but hardly anyone is, and this was quite upsetting to me. Long story short, we purchased on the spot a very unique, quite expensive (we thought at the time), interesting, talking-walking device we hadn't seen before so we could make these waters at home. I am joking. The machine did talk in several languages, but it wasn't walking. I particularly liked the water which removed all the pesticides and carcinogens from the produce. Because of my compromised immune system, I was desperate to avoid as many chemicals and metals as possible. We borrowed the money for this health machine, as we had none.

I was faithfully drinking tons of water as it was easy to keep up. I never felt bloated. In three months, all the different aches and pains I'd had for years went away and I never had to deal with a bladder infection again. My "thirst signal" turned back on, after not feeling thirsty for decades. The muscle spasms stopped and my brain started working again, and this was the most amazing change I noticed. Having unusually sharp and clear thoughts to which I wasn't accustomed, I was getting everything done in no time. I could focus better than ever before and my memory improved 100%. Reducing the number of supplements to a third, including the 800 mg/day of magnesium I had to take before, saved us money. I loved having all this new energy which lasted all day. I slept like a baby. I could easily drink four liters daily, which was a miracle in itself. I gained a zest for life once again, and turned into the happiest version of myself. In a few weeks, something else happened completely unexpectedly, and it was major: my husband quit drinking soda! It was hard to believe it, as I have tried to get him off these poisons many times before but I couldn't get anywhere. My daughter started to take water from us and stopped drinking Diet Coke in less than a month. Her mood changed substantially and to my great surprise, she started exercising. She was quite a couch potato when she moved from Toronto to BC, and now like an energizer bunny, she started to do Zumba, stairs, and yoga. In a year she lost forty pounds even though she stayed with her usual diet, which wasn't bad, aside from the soda. This made me the happiest mother on Earth.

In about eight months all my symptoms disappeared, and Fred dropped his meds and had normal test results in six months! This led to another $250 in monthly savings. In a short time, this fabulous "health machine" solved so many issues for us that I had to dive deep into the research of this technology. I found a long history and an exciting international effort that not many know about. For decades, tons of research was happening but most of it was done remotely, and the discoveries were phenomenal! They changed society's understanding of water, however this new information never got out to the masses. I read everything I could find and concluded that the science of Electrolyzed Reduced Water (ERW) is rock solid! This water is used and endorsed by truly eminent doctors and top experts worldwide who have nothing to hide and nothing to gain. I found no gimmicks or BS. More importantly, we started hearing incredible testimonials from people we shared water with, which had a tremendous effect on me, as I believe in actual results before any "science" which I know can be corrupted just like everything else.

We opened a fancy B&B at the time and we called it Ryder Lake Lodge. Two of our guests bought the device after drinking the water for only a few days. One morning in 2013, I woke up with the realization that we needed to close the business and start talking to people who I knew were suffering! It became clear to me that this water would be the ultimate solution for many people, a very practical and affordable one, and I wanted to bring it to them.

In a few months, I could drive and work again in my insurance business, but by then we fell behind with mortgage payments and the bank wouldn't accept the money retroactively. We lost the house. It wasn't easy to leave our gorgeous chalet-style home on a beautiful piece of land on the hill, surrounded by cedars. We walked out with zero dollars just because a realtor sold the property for $300,000 below market and appraised value! That was our equity, and the sale was illegal as we found out later... Surprisingly, though, I was at peace; all I could think about was this therapeutic water and the people we could help with it. I gave up my insurance license to focus on learning a new, very different trade at age 60. Normal people don't do that of course, but I have never been afraid of unusual things or situations. We struggled for a couple of years, and then our new business exploded. I started to travel. It wasn't hard, because I felt better than when I was forty. Now at 70, I have great hips and knees to walk, skate, or jump while playing pickleball. I never had to get hip surgery; I hydrated my joints, and **that is all I did.** I never bought into the collagen theory, either. When I tell people how I replaced the possible hip replacements with water, I can see their disbelief. It has been twelve years since I began managing my health at home, on my own, with my water, and I do not take any medication. As long as I am drinking enough, I feel great. The "hemiblock," which is a faulty electrical conduction of the arteries, and the doctors have no answer for, somehow gets corrected by this electrically charged water loaded with organic mineral salts and

I can have a normal life. No more running to the emergency for me. This is the most magical thing I have ever experienced. It's a real blast not to depend on the system!

* * * *

Great health should be the norm, but many are struggling with balance, flexibility, lack of energy, pain, knee/hip replacements, diabetes, neurodegenerative conditions, auto-immune problems, sleeping and digestive issues, migraines, or cancer. People are looking for relief in all the wrong places! Only a few understand that hydration should come before diet and exercise. With all the enormous advancements in the last 100 years in every other field, why is health the only area in which we are going backward? Why are so many people who eat well are malnourished or toxic? Could it be the lack of functional water? Sean Stratton, a famous nutritionist, says: "*What you can utilize matters more than what you eat!*" Some spend top dollar on expensive natural/organic foods, not understanding that the nutrients might never get into their cells where they can be utilized if they are not drinking functional water, which is the only means of transportation of the nutrients! The cell water is where all the chemical reactions take place. According to new information by whistleblowers, both cancer and dementia are metabolic diseases, pointing to cell metabolism.

Most of the doctors and experts on neurotransmitters know nothing, or not enough, about the number one nutrient, which is water!

A scientific study on human volunteers published in the United States by a famous cardiologist shows that cell metabolism, mitochondria, ATP production, and platelet production in the blood were all significantly enhanced by ERW! Drinking this type of water leads to measurably greater antioxidant capacity, reduction in inflammation, improved recovery after injury, **and readiness for stress-induced damage repair.** I think this is huge. No, I know this is huge… The question is, will anyone listen to a humble opinion? This can make the difference, or determine if someone dies or survives and recovers in case of a stroke or a heart attack! In fact, we saw this over and over again in our circles.

Tap water, well water, sodas, marketed drinks, and "purified waters" are dead waters, so broken that filtration won't restore the water's structure or functionality. This means that these waters won't absorb and hydrate. When one is drinking bulk water, about fifteen percent will absorb. The Nobel laureate Albert Szent-Gyorgyi, the genius behind Vitamin C, states; *The molecular structure of the water is the essence of life. Who will change that structure in the living systems will change the world.* Scientists today agree that the structure of the water is more important than the chemical composition, simply because the structure of the water together with its negative electrical charge is what makes the water functional. What I am trying to say is this: The bulk water you have access to is only good to wash dishes and to flush toilets, not so much for hydration! Bottled waters are not only dead and full of carcinogens but have plastic particles that can interfere with blood flow; 80% of people now have these in their blood, and that makes some experts very worried. Plastic is especially dangerous for men, causing an epidemic, as it mimics the female hormone estrogen! *The Disappearing Male* is a mind-blowing and eye-opening documentary that everyone should be aware of.

* * * *

By reading books, tons of literature, and peer-reviewed studies, and researching the subject day and night for six years, my eyes were opened. Experiencing cellular dehydration, plus the clinical data I found, made me realize that yes, Dr. Batmanghelidj, this genius of a doctor, was right; dehydration is indeed the real cancer of today's society and conventional, modern medicine is quiet about it. His amazing books are eye opening and life changing.

"Dehydration is causing inflammation and oxidative stress," they say. True, but this is only a drop in an ocean-size story, yet the following is the most you will find when you research it: *"Dehydration 'appears' prevalent, costly, associated with adverse outcomes, poses a risk to public health, **is underrecognized and is poorly managed! Further research is required to improve the assessment and 'management' of dehydration,"*** according to a recent consensus on the subject.

Why manage it? Why not solve it, or eliminate it all together? Why not tell the truth as it is? When will this "further research" happen? Chances are, never, and that is why I am speaking out…consider me a whistleblower! Most people are unaware of it, just like I was. Even when they hear it, they don't believe it, because conventional medicine does not acknowledge simple facts. They call it Dry-Nose Syndrome, Dry-Eyes Syndrome, Dry-Everything Syndrome, or give the condition a ridiculous label like "Stiff Person Syndrome" (please look up Celine Dion, who is in critical condition), as these have nothing to do with dehydration. Insanity! All this nonsense is just fear-mongering by a failing system to make things more complicated than they need to be. There are no warnings or education on this subject, so is it relevant? What do you think? With 50 million people having "autoimmune diseases" in the USA alone, and the same happening all over the world, why not look further into the issue? After all, it is one of the largest causes of disability in women. It takes doctors between three and five years to diagnose it. And what then? Do they have a magic cure, or any cure? Autoimmune and chronic conditions are not diseases we "catch," and pills won't fix them. The immune system is the biggest gift we receive from before birth, and we should strengthen it with proper nutrition and lifestyle while growing up. It will turn against us if we don't take care of it. We don't respect our creator when we are not taking good care of this amazing operating system he planted in us. It can be fibromyalgia, diabetes, cancer, or lupus; it does not matter.

* * * *

"To solve a difficult problem in medicine, don't study it directly, but rather pursue a curiosity about nature and the rest will follow."
—Roger Kornberg PhD. Stanford School of Medicine

So, what are we missing, or perhaps ignoring, in this era of toxic chemicals led by Big Pharma? Here it is, this is what I learned: We are electrical beings, meaning that our body's natural electrical charge has to be maintained at all costs to stay healthy, or alive for that matter. Our cells operate at -22 mV. For the body to heal, fight inflammation, and make healthy new cells, a minimum of -50 mV of charge is required. This must be obtained from the body's hydrogen bank (water), electrolyte minerals (a minimum of 54% of which has to come from water), and organic anti-oxidants. The body's sensitive pH balance has to be maintained as well, in order for the immune system to work and to prevent imbalance, or dis-ease! Water which naturally has a high pH is by far the easiest way to achieve this! Hydration at a cellular level also must be maintained. Being 70% water, lack of hydration leads to a low electrical charge, hydrogen depletion, fatigue/low energy, and acidosis (lack of oxygen in the blood and the body), due to the accumulation of toxins in the cells. Researchers like the Romanian father of fluid dynamics, Henry Coanda, discovered the three most vital biomarkers of water. These are its electrical charge, its naturally high pH, and the small clustered structure. These are the properties of nature's water which will create homeostasis in all living beings, as this water can recharge our cells by donating electrons, keeping the hydration levels and the pH balance! There is much more to tissue hydration than simply drinking ordinary water. When your water is "tested," all you get is the components (sulphates, metals, minerals, pathogens, additives, etc.). No one understands or cares whether your water is functional or therapeutic. Chances are, you've never even heard about this research, mainly because water is a natural element so it can't be patented, meaning no one can make money! I meet people all the time who are drinking tons of water and they are not getting hydrated. The most dehydrated people are the athletes, dancers, and singers. Dehydration is the main cause of concussions, lactic acid buildup, most injuries, and long recovery time. Everyone should know the difference between dead water and living water! They are like night and day! Most beverages and coffee have a dehydrating effect, contributing to the sad situation humanity finds itself in.

No doctor who pretends to know everything on YouTube (there are a few) or anywhere else, has a solution for mineral deficiencies, other than recommending iron, calcium or magnesium pills. They never talk about the root cause of chronic conditions, period. They promote those supplements as the cause and the solution, but mineral deficiency is also only a symptom! The root cause is a lack of water, causing dehydration, acidosis and lack of natural minerals (electrolytes)! When you know the root cause, you have the solution!

I think here lies the answer to why I suffered so much for decades when I wasn't drinking water: The water available today is dead, with an acidic pH, and a positive Oxidation Reduction Potential (between +300 and +500), so it is oxidizing and creating more free radicals in the body. It seems that it does the exact opposite of what it should be doing. It won't absorb either, it has over twenty or even thirty molecules stuck together in huge clusters. The water sent to me by an angel who goes by the name of Sabine, and which I am still drinking today, twelve years later, has a negative voltage, it donates millions of electrons, just like nature's water, and therefore is an antioxidant. It is alkalizing with a naturally high pH (9.5, with nothing added), loaded with colloidal minerals from the source water that my body can use and has a small hexagonal structure (only six molecules per cluster), so it absorbs instantly into the cells.

A dehydrated brain won't perform well, as the brain is the most affected of all the organs. Due to a dehydrated brain, people lose their minds (they panic, are aggressive or depressed), they compromise their memory, their focus, and even their judgment! Dehydration is often labelled as "dementia!" What a tragedy! People in their fifties are given meds, making their situation even worse! Fred and I have no problem focusing and reading for hours and hours every day. I think the water plays a tremendous role in this. It took me over three years, however, to catch up with hydration. It felt like I was given new lungs and a new brain. Now, I am ready to start university! I am looking forward to the future, and I don't care if this sounds crazy to people of similar ages looking at old age homes. It took Fred over five years to hydrate his grossly dehydrated body.

Anxiety and depression are linked to the intestinal flora. The "microbiome" is called the "second brain" for a reason! We know now that there is no such thing as "chemical imbalance" in the brain! This nonsense was sold to us for decades! How much responsibility does the water have in this case? You be the judge: *"Organochlorines and other additives to tap water will suppress the immune functions, will destroy the intestinal flora, and can cause mutations by altering the DNA..."* Health Canada says. Notice the contrast: In 1965 (that was a long time ago!), the Ministry of Health and Welfare in Japan announced, *"The permanent intake of ERW is effective for the restoration of the intestinal flora!"* This is just one of the reasons why over 400 hospitals in Japan use ERW.

So, what do you think? Is the population sick and sad by design, or because they want to be ill? Neither, of course! They are ill and depressed for the same reason; they are thirsty, starving, toxic, and acidic. They are bombarded with processed foods, marketed drinks and GMO waters to which their bodies react naturally. Period.

* * * *

I came across a book called *Brain on Fire*, telling the true story of an American reporter. I was practically drawn to this book at an airport. When I read it, I couldn't believe it! What happened to the heroine in the story is a 100% replica of a period of my life. A motion picture was also produced based on this book. Her story reveals a crisis caused by chronic dehydration. This is an important story! By going through this myself, I ironically know more about it than the doctors treating this young journalist. Susannah Callahan goes through an absolute ordeal. A weird event is interrupting her life and her work, and no one including her doctors can find what is causing the seizures and hallucinations. She had no precedent or any illness. Up to this point, Susannah and I had the same experience. In her case, however, specialists went as far as a brain biopsy, which is a three-hour surgery to find out why her brain was "on fire." The doctors could not find the cause of it, however, and with their wrong perspective, they never will. A bit of common sense would help, but her doctors had the "complicated mind syndrome."

This was a combination of living on coffee (which dehydrates and robs your body of minerals, especially magnesium), no sleep (she was over-stressed), and not drinking water. The very reason why she could not handle stress or sleep was that her brain became dehydrated almost beyond the point of return. She wasn't feeling good and she kept drinking coffee. Her brain couldn't handle the crisis caused by the primary stress of dehydration. Hydration is always the primary stressor. Firefighters know what to do when something catches on fire, but brain specialists in the US could not figure out how to help this poor woman! Weeks of investigation went nowhere. Her parents were worried sick and no one had a clue what was happening. No cause was found! Eventually, she did recover by hydrating intravenously, I think. Her "condition" was given a new label. We know that thousands of these labels circulate in the sick air of different hospitals and medical clinics.

They mean mostly nothing...the story ends with a huge question mark...

Not for me! Not sleeping and being dehydrated is an extremely dangerous combination. You start having seizures and hallucinating, or vice-versa.

How do I know this? Once again, I learned this unfortunately by experience. I am ashamed to admit it, but it is true. I spent two weeks at St. Joseph Hospital in Toronto in the "loonie bin" because of an identical episode. I was tied down, not sure for how long, but I remember the hallucinations as if they happened yesterday. At this point, I wasn't sleeping, nor drinking much water for two weeks. Not many have experienced this, in my humble opinion. The world record now is eleven days. I did not sleep for fourteen days and nights. The hallucinations seemed real and were so vivid that I chose to pee in my bed as I was convinced that the washroom was a gas chamber. Thankfully, God granted me an older and amazing doctor, a rare find, who knew what he was doing. He gave me enough aid to sleep for two weeks. Thank you, Dr. Jeney, for saving my life. I am wondering— how many people are put on drugs for a long period (or permanently) and getting labelled as "psychotics" because of clinical dehydration?

Those were tough times...I lost my job, which we depended on financially; I lost beautiful relationships, and so much more. Related to this incident I also experienced the effects of psychotic drugs, taking them temporarily after the incident. I was drugged for five months, therefore completely out of circulation. Only by the grace of God am I here today. When I cried out, he gave me the wisdom to call my doctor while I was planning to jump off the fourteenth floor. I was so close...I walked out to the balcony in my Toronto apartment to make sure that I was falling on concrete and not grass, so I would die for sure. I know it wasn't me...I never wanted to die! During the biggest battles of my life, not once did I think about suicide. The pills were messing with my brain. When I called my doctor, he immediately knew what was going on… He managed to talk me out of jumping and he took me off the drug…so I lived.

This is why I am certain that these meds cause suicidal thoughts or an "urge" to commit suicide, which is almost *impossible* to resist! Most suicides are drug-induced! They have nothing to do with the person wanting to die. I can't pretend that I don't know all this, especially because this heinous crime is going on now more than ever!

* * * *

I hope you agree that after all this, it is not surprising that I realized early on how vital good quality, functional water is. It is a matter of survival, as regular water is not drinkable, nor is it desirable anymore. Being able to distribute such necessities worldwide with no competition is every salesperson's dream come true. So, at age 60, I closed my insurance business because I knew I found gold along with never-before-experienced satisfaction and joy. To this day I continue to discuss dehydration at my webinars, in my books, and at every opportunity I get, in every country I visit. Dehydration happened to me in such a big way that it turned me into the poster child of involuntary cellular dehydration. This is one label I accept. The bright side of this ordeal was that it created a micro-niche for me, where I might just be one of the most knowledgeable people on the subject, and that is sweeeet! The grace that was poured on me is much more than I deserve. This girl needed water, and the best water was sent to her by divine intervention.

> *"Grace is finding a waterfall when you were only*
> *looking for a stream."*
> —Vanessa Hunt

It took me ten years of hard work to achieve success. It is a privilege to be a world ambassador for this sustainable water and eco-friendly lifestyle, but I did not do it alone. I had the support and sacrificial help of my husband and partner, and the help of my sponsors, Roger and Sabine, for years. We did it together. It is a great blessing to have this knowledge, no matter how hard it was to go through this experience. In my wildest dreams I never imagined that I would be in a position to teach others about chronic dehydration. I am often called not only by individuals, but also by medical doctors, naturopaths, and other practitioners from all over the globe to explain the unique properties of this water, why it works so well, how to achieve extraordinary results, and how it is produced. They are coming to us through the clinics, spas, and healthcare providers we are working with. Even ionized waters aren't the same. Some are only ionized to a certain degree and the results aren't great.

Thankfully, many doctors are waking up to the fact that water brought back to its natural state is superior to pharmaceuticals. I wish that people would realize the irrevocable truth that nature alone offers relief, health, and happiness to humankind, and that, therefore, we have to cherish it, in many instances restore it, and preserve it for the next generations. The only "side effect" of this amazing water is looking and feeling younger! I am not kidding. The hydrogen gas (H2) abundant in this antioxidant water is considered not only "the future of medicine," but is indeed the missing link to longevity!

The reason I am healthy today is because I embraced this electrolyzed water (very different from "alkaline water," which is a scam) and I am doing my best to stay away from the landmines hidden in our foods, meds, skin care products, medical treatments, etc. Some of the world's most powerful corporations are constantly coming up with new traps and new poisons in deceptive forms. It is impossible to survive nowadays unless we are aware of these things, so we can exercise

"Biological Self-Defence!" In the last four decades, I became a "medical spy" just to stay alive. This is why I am convinced that natural immunity is the only way to go! This is what I believe, practice, and teach with love and compassion. Please allow me to close with a quote you might not like, but you might need:

> *"We can ignore reality, but we cannot ignore*
> *the consequences of ignoring reality!"*
> —Ayn Rand

Darlene Oliver

Sweet Home Launch Business Coaching
Serial Entrepreneur, Author, Coach, and Work from Home Guru

https://www.linkedin.com/in/darlenekoliver/
https://www.facebook.com/SweetHomeLaunchBusinessCoaching
https://www.instagram.com/kaydoliver/
https://www.mompreneurssweetspot.com/
https://realworkfromhomejobsandbusinessopportunities.com/

Darlene stands as a beacon of innovation and resilience in the work-from-home domain, leveraging personal challenges to fuel her entrepreneurial quest. Celebrated for her revolutionary "Triple E Framework," she has carved a niche guiding mothers and entrepreneurs to start a business and propel their ventures to success. Her methodology, spotlighted in Home Business Magazine and various influential platforms including The Work From Home Forever Podcast and Stories Of Hope, reveals a practical blueprint for navigating adversity while fostering entrepreneurship. As an acclaimed author, serial entrepreneur, mentor, and work from home Guru, Darlene credits divine inspiration for her accomplishments, dedicating her life to unlocking others' potential. The cornerstone of her mission is MompreneursSweetSpot.com, a community she cultivates with passion, empowering startups and entrepreneurs to transform dreams into tangible achievements. Her work exemplifies a commitment to guiding aspiring mompreneurs with expertise, faith-driven resilience, and a heart for entrepreneurship.

BEYOND THE ROLLERCOASTER: UNVEILING GOD'S PLAN AMIDST LIFE'S CHALLENGES AND JOYS

By Darlene Oliver

Life has a knack for throwing curveballs, but here's the secret: You hold the power to step up your game. As we navigate this rollercoaster called life, we're not alone; divine providence guides us, and challenges become stepping stones for growth. Imperfect as we are, God crafted each of us with purpose. Through our faith, we draw strength, even in moments of uncertainty.

With God as our ally, we confront obstacles head-on, knowing His plans surpass our understanding. Let's embrace our humanity, lean into His guidance, and march forward with unwavering faith.

So fasten your seatbelt, my friend, as I invite you on a thrilling journey through my story of growth, resilience, and remarkable achievements. Together, let's learn to defy the odds and seize every opportunity for personal triumph that God has planned for us.

When I was little, I was brimming with joy, innocence, and a love for God, but I was oblivious to the trials that lay ahead. Little did I know the darkness that would eventually seep into my life. Let me tell you a story about my early years. It was a rollercoaster ride, with the intermittent presence of our alcoholic father and the courageous decision my mother made to divorce him. At just twenty-eight, she took on the responsibility of raising four small children alone, with no support from family, friends, or the community.

The devil continued to play his mischievous games in our lives; he had an arsenal of challenges ready for us. Just when my mother believed she had discovered her knight in shining armor, little did she suspect it was only the introduction to a twisted childhood story woven with the threads of abuse. As if that weren't sufficient, we were an unruly bunch that transformed our home into a tumultuous rollercoaster, where dull moments were nonexistent.

We faced financial struggles, too. Even though they both worked two jobs at times, my mother and stepdad struggled to make ends meet. I'll never forget the year when our utilities were shut off and we lived without them for three months during the summer. But you know what? We made the best of it. Homework under the captivating glow of streetlights felt like a thrilling secret adventure, and cooking meals on a barbecue grill was like a perpetual summer campout for four young, adventurous children. Those experiences shaped who I am today.

Years later, my mother sent us to live with my biological father who had a new family and had quit drinking. Unfortunately, although he no longer drank, he was abusive. Although my twin and I ended up returning to live with our mom again a few months later, my younger siblings were left in a similar situation to the one they had left. Our relationship with our younger siblings has suffered as a result, and is still suffering forty-something years later.

As for my twin and me, we stayed with our mom. However, life took a different turn for each of us. My twin got married at the tender age of 17 and welcomed her first child shortly after. I was jealous of her at the time because it seemed she was happy and loved, but she ended up being abused by her husband for years before leaving him. Looking back, I now understand we were all stuck in a cycle that needed to be broken, and we eventually did with God's help, but it took many years.

I left home on my eighteenth birthday, but quickly found myself on the streets, drinking and selling myself. Then life threw me another curveball: I became pregnant with my first child that year and had to rely on government aid. Despite the difficulties, I was overjoyed with having a child. However, let me tell you, scarcity and abuse didn't just affect us—they infiltrated every crevice of our existence.

It wasn't just about the abuse, or the scarcity itself. It changed the way we saw the world and ourselves, giving birth to this bizarre scarcity mentality that whispered doubts about deserving anything or anyone good. And oh boy, my confidence took a major hit, too, leaving me feeling unlovable and unworthy! But here's the kicker: Those experiences shaped me in ways I never saw coming.

Life's curveballs may have caught me off guard, but with God by my side, I found the strength to rise above. Each obstacle became an opportunity to deepen my reliance on Him and to discover and become the person I was meant to be. Through the highs and lows, I clung to the assurance that God's hand was guiding me, shaping me into the individual He envisioned.

As I continued on my journey to find my true calling, I encountered the first toxic relationship to trip me up, but the pure joy of being a mother filled my heart. When that marriage ended because of my husband's cocaine addiction, me and my five children picked up the pieces and started to rebuild our lives. Jobs came and went, yet a yearning deep down inside persisted. I felt a voice telling me that I was made for more.

Moreover, I developed an unwavering dedication to providing my kids with a life beyond my own experiences. Let me tell you, it was no easy journey. Nevertheless, I couldn't help but strive for an unseen goal, pushing myself to become the best version of me, not only for my own sake, but also for the sake of my children. And you want to know something? My children transformed into my driving force, my ultimate inspiration.

Becoming a parent was a transformative experience for me. However, what surprised me the most was witnessing the same mindset I had struggled with being passed down to my children. Despite my tireless efforts to infuse them with confidence and self-belief, they found themselves grappling with the same doubts and fears that once had, and still, haunted me. It felt like a never-ending cycle of progress, setbacks, and new obstacles that knocked me down, plunging me into a familiar abyss of uncertainty and doubt time and time again. And, as if echoing my battles, my children faced their own trials and tribulations. They inherited my mindset by witnessing my battles. And let me tell you, it wasn't a smooth journey!

Deep down inside of me, a tiny yet unwavering voice kept whispering that I possessed boundless potential. It was an elusive sensation, tantalizingly close, with the prospect of unlocking a life far beyond my current circumstances. I was fully aware that seizing this opportunity was not only crucial for my own journey, but was also a powerful way to inspire my children, proving to them that they, too, could accomplish the extraordinary. Oh, how I longed to liberate myself and my family from this relentless cycle and present my precious kids with a chance to embrace an entirely different future brimming with infinite possibilities.

When I ran away at 18, I had just dropped out of school like a rebel. But life has a funny way of showing you what truly matters. Now, as a parent with an insatiable hunger for greatness, I knew I had to get serious about education. No way was I going to move up in the world without heading back to school. So, with determination coursing through my veins, I took the plunge and enrolled in college. My initial dream was just to get my associate's degree. Little did I know that God had something better in mind.

During my time in school, I thrived and relished every moment, uncovering hidden passions for writing and astronomy. It was a journey of self-discovery, showcasing my true capabilities. I even soared with a 4.0 GPA for several semesters, until the mighty challenge of "Economy 101" came along. Phew! Let me clarify, the 4.0 wasn't a result of trying too hard; I simply reveled in the classes and flourished within that stimulating atmosphere. God was paving the way for my future by offering opportunities that helped me finish my degree, and I was soaking knowledge up like a sponge knowing that I would use it in the future.

After graduation, I enthusiastically set off on a captivating adventure, eager to unravel the mysteries that awaited me. It didn't take long before a thrilling opportunity crossed my path, igniting a fire of excitement and anticipation within me. Surpassing all expectations, I thrived in the role, swiftly rising to the occasion and earning a promotion within just a few months. Not only was I promoted, but I was also entrusted with leading a whole department. Quite the journey, wouldn't you agree?

But something was still missing. Throughout my career journey, as I climbed the corporate ladder, I couldn't shake the feeling of emptiness. Sure, there were moments of triumph, but at what cost? Sacrificing precious time with my loved ones, pouring countless hours into someone else's vision, struggling to make ends meet, and dealing with the sting of unexpected layoffs and crappy relationships... It all made me question the true purpose of everything. I yearned for more control over my destiny, more freedom in my professional life, and more peace in my circumstances.

It was about this time that I hit another detour. I met a man who later became my husband, and a true departure from the course I should have been on. It was the beginning of a rocky relationship that would end badly. Not long after marrying my husband, I suffered another job loss, and that's when I decided to take a leap of faith and chase after my dreams.

It became clear that a change was long overdue. It was time to embark on a transformative expedition toward a path filled with fulfillment and meaning. It was in a moment of audacity, after being laid off from yet another job, that I sold my home and used the equity to buy a brick-and-mortar business. But here's the twist—even though I dove headfirst into entrepreneurship, putting myself into debt, I was not enjoying anything about what I was doing, not making the money I had hoped, and I was working a grueling 60 hours a week, which was a reality far from what I had expected.

I had boldly purchased an established landscaping business, envisioning a harmonious collaboration with my husband. Little did I know, the path to success would be paved with unexpected challenges. My husband, who had a bad temper, was not prepared for business ownership, and he quickly began to have conflicts with me and the employees. Then, dealing with untrustworthy employees stealing clients while on the clock added fuel to the fire of our woes.

I found myself out in the field, sleeves rolled up, tackling maintenance work, fixing sprinklers, overseeing the crew with my husband during the day, and doing office work at night. Both physically and mentally drained, the toll of manual labor weighed heavy on my shoulders. Meanwhile, my marriage was already on rocky ground, my husband's temper was getting worse, he was drinking and doing drugs, and he wasn't getting along with my children. The combination of money problems and business struggles only added to the strain. I knew this was not what God intended for me.

What I once hoped would be a thriving venture turned into a profit-diminishing, time-consuming nightmare. Stress consumed me, and my bank account wasn't reflecting the anticipated rewards. My marriage was a mess, and my children were feeling all of the stress and conflict, too. As a matter of fact, it seemed like failure, a detour from my true path as a business owner, mother, and child of God. Overwhelmed and disheartened, I questioned my choices as I became depressed and suicidal.

Deep inside, I knew there had to be a better way, one that aligned with the life I was meant for. I knew what I had to do. The road ahead was unclear, but I summoned up every ounce of courage and made some bold moves. I separated from my husband and sold the business. I had decided to return to my corporate career, determined to find my true path and create a life of peace for my family.

It didn't take long for me to stumble upon another job opportunity. Determined to alter my fortunes, I made the bold decision to embark on another adventurous journey back to school to pursue my bachelor's degree. With a mix of excitement and skepticism, I wholeheartedly embraced the Bellevue University experience, wondering if it would truly impact my career. Despite the uncertainties, this pursuit became a remarkable milestone that reignited my self-belief, even if it was for a fleeting moment.

Now, at this point in my life, I already had five adorable children that I loved with all my heart from previous relationships, and I thought my baby-making days were long gone. Fate, however, had a delightful curveball ready for me. Surprise, surprise! At the age of 42, with my marriage at an end, I found myself with a bun in the oven! Talk about a shocker! I had been told that there was very little chance I would have another child and that it was not recommended. The fact that I got pregnant at all was a near miracle which gave me a glimpse of a better future. I knew this gift was from God and this unexpected twist only fueled my determination to be a better version of myself.

Soon after, life dealt me a severe blow—I lost my job yet again around the time of my youngest daughter's birth. It felt like a never-ending cycle of disappointment. Months passed, and despite the tireless effort

I put into my job search, I remained unemployed, drowning in debt, and scared for my family's future.

Just when I thought things couldn't get worse, fate played another cruel trick on me. I found myself caught in a major accident, completely helpless and vulnerable with permanent injuries and in pain. Facing the challenge of motherhood alone was already overwhelming, but as if that wasn't enough, my ex-husband, the father of my baby, was deported, leaving me to navigate this daunting journey on my own. Honestly, he wouldn't have been much help even if he had been around, but his absence made it crystal clear just how alone I was.

Fear gripped my heart, and the future seemed hazy, like a puzzle with missing pieces. How was I going to rebuild my shattered life while providing for my beloved children? I remember coming home one day to unexpectedly find a lock on the front door to my home, and realized it was being foreclosed with my belongings still inside. It left me wondering what I was to do. As my finances plummeted at an alarming rate, I was left with no other option but to file for bankruptcy. It was undeniably the darkest chapter of my existence, where despair clouded my every thought.

During this perplexing phase of my life, my twin sister emerged as my champion. With only two children left in my care—my baby and her high school graduate older sister—I made the bold decision to move in with my sister and her family. The prospect of determining the course of my future seemed daunting, and I felt overwhelmed, useless, and adrift. But hold on, let me share something extraordinary with you. It was precisely during this rock-bottom moment that I stumbled upon the long-awaited breakthrough I had sought throughout my life. Trust me, this tale is bound to captivate you!

Picture this: I had absolutely nothing left to lose—my pride, my self-confidence, it had all vanished into thin air. But then, out of the blue, my sister had this crazy idea of starting our own home-based businesses. At first, my past failures flooded my every thought, my scarcity mindset and lack of confidence and faith wanted to hold me back, and boy, they were so very damned persistent. But deep down, a voice kept telling me that I couldn't let those demons control my life forever. I felt a persistent nudge, and I knew I could not ignore it. It was time for an epic showdown. I had waited long enough to reveal who I was meant to be and I had to find out who that person was, no matter what it took.

I still remember the moment when it hit me—like a lightning bolt of realization. It wasn't just about shaping my own future, you know? It was about carving a path for my beloved kids and grandkids, too. Breaking free from the clutches of scarcity and self-doubt became my top priority because my family deserved nothing less than complete liberation. That life-altering moment became the spark, the catalyst for action. With every ounce of courage I had left, I shouted a resounding "Yes!"

Launching my very own home-based business became an act of defiance, a rebellion against letting circumstances, and this cruel world, define who I am or control me. Over the years, I've amassed quite an impressive collection of books and attended countless programs, all in pursuit of success as an entrepreneur. But you know what? More often than not, I found myself wavering and hesitating when golden opportunities came knocking at my door. My feelings of fear, self-doubt, and inadequacy kept whispering in my mind that I would fail…and I listened when I shouldn't have.

Let me tell you what set this attempt apart. It was my unyielding tenacity and determination to push ahead, even in the face of adversity. It was my faith that God was guiding my path, and I absolutely refused to give up or settle for the ordinary in the face of the extraordinary that I knew God had waiting for me.

I became a force to be reckoned with, even if failure was a possibility. You see, not taking a chance on myself was simply out of the question. This empowered mindset enabled me to conquer every challenge that dared to cross my path, all while seizing exciting opportunities along the way. Get ready, because this journey is about to get real!

Ever since that defining moment, my life has taken an amazing twist for the better. I've had the incredible privilege of delving into a whopping 15 different job titles, all while basking in the comforts of my own home. The cherry on top? I get to call the shots on what I do, how I do it, and how much I rake in. Throughout this extraordinary journey, I've fine-tuned and enriched my skills and knowledge with utmost precision. And guess what?

It all led me to a game-changing decision—to share my triumphs and experiences. At first, it was a pro bono effort. But when I realized the profound impact I could have by reaching out to more folks, I made it my mission to share my expertise and skills through books and by being a trusted coach, just for folks like you.

Now, as I reflect on my journey, I see the fingerprints of God's grace and mercy in every triumph and every setback. His presence was my constant companion, illuminating the path ahead and instilling within me the courage to press on. With unwavering faith, I embraced the challenges, knowing that they were refining me, molding me into the person God intended. I was not perfect, and I made many mistakes, but God's patience rivals his love, and he did not give up on me.

So, as I share my story of growth, resilience, and unimaginable achievements, I do so with a heart overflowing with gratitude. For I know that behind it all, God was orchestrating every moment, leading me closer to His purpose for my life. And in the end, I stand as a testament to the power of faith, for God was there every step of the way…even when I doubted it.

As a result of the unique experiences God has graciously allowed me to encounter, I've gleaned a profound lesson: With unwavering faith in God's guidance, coupled with resolute determination, any dream can be realized. It all begins with a firm belief in oneself and the courage to take decisive action. As I reflect on my journey, I am compelled to share this invaluable insight with others, for I believe it is my divine calling to empower them to embrace boundless success.

Hence, I've meticulously crafted the Triple E Framework, with God's help, to serve as a transformative tool for individuals seeking to break free from self-imposed limitations. Through this framework, I aspire to assist others in unlocking their true potential, enabling them to soar to unprecedented heights.

I've uncovered a profound truth that I feel compelled to impart—greatness in life is not reserved for the select few deemed geniuses; rather, it is an attainable state for every individual who dares to believe in the power of God's plan for their life and takes bold steps to manifest it. The key lies in embracing audacity and unwavering resilience, trusting in God's providence as we navigate life's relentless challenges.

To those grappling with self-doubt or a scarcity mindset, I urge you to anchor yourselves firmly in your faith and the boundless potential that God has instilled within you. Never relent in the pursuit of your dreams, for within each of us lies the spark of greatness, awaiting its moment to illuminate the world. Believe me, my dear friend, with God's guidance, anything is possible.

Curious about how I kickstarted my home-based business? Wondering how you can replicate this success in your own life? I'm thrilled to share my journey and provide you with the tools you need to embark on your own entrepreneurial adventure because I want each and every reader to be able to experience the joy and freedom I felt as a business owner. So get ready to dive into the extraordinary world of entrepreneurship as I unveil the powerful methodology that propelled me forward so you can make giant strides too. Brace yourself for an empowering journey that will ignite greatness in your business endeavors!

I used The Triple E Framework:
Expertise + Emotions + Earning = Success!

Are you ready to take the reins of your business and thrive as a confident, successful entrepreneur? If your desire to achieve financial stability is fierce, and you're determined to steer clear of common pitfalls, then lean in! Get ready to dive into the exhilarating realm of entrepreneurial pursuit as we uncover the top three mistakes entrepreneurs make and how the Triple E Framework can empower you to overcome these missteps and launch your dream business.

Now, here's the scoop: Starting a business can be a wild ride, especially when it comes to finding your perfect fit. Many aspiring entrepreneurs embark on their dream voyage only to be faced with unresolved challenges, meager earnings, and an overall sense of dissatisfaction that prompts them to question their initial motivations.

Fear not! I am here to equip you with the ultimate key to success in building your own business. This tried-and-true methodology will expertly navigate you away from the treacherous pitfalls that often befall entrepreneurs. Curious to know what these notorious mistakes are?

Allow me to enlighten you:

- First and foremost, many entrepreneurs start a business without the necessary expertise.

- Secondly, many entrepreneurs neglect to consider the profound impact of emotions on their journey to triumph.

- And last but not least, many fail to maximize their earning potential to unlock ultimate success.

Feeling a tad overwhelmed? Don't be! The Triple E Framework will help you in launching a business where you become the unrivaled expert, carve your path doing what you love, and generate good earnings.

And there's more! By embracing my approach, you will unlock an abundance of additional benefits and rewards along your entrepreneurial journey. So, if you're a passionate aspiring entrepreneur seeking a transformative change, keep reading! Prepare to witness how The Triple E Framework can help you navigate your business venture to success while sidestepping the top three mistakes that entrepreneurs make.

Being a business owner requires more than just knowledge; it demands expertise.

To truly flourish in your business, you must possess the necessary experience, problem-solving capabilities, and the ability to inspire confidence in yourself and your customers. Lack of experience, skills, or knowledge can only erode trust, hinder your performance, and result in costly mistakes. Such setbacks jeopardize your business and its clientele. They also sow self-doubt, affecting both you and your customers. You will not have faith in yourself, and your customers will not have faith in you either.

So, in this fast-paced market where ignorance is not bliss but a recipe for disaster, how do you find an opportunity that aligns with your expertise? The first step toward a successful business venture is identifying and analyzing your skills. Knowing your strengths and weaknesses will give you a competitive edge and help you find your niche in the market. Let's explore a few ways you can identify and analyze your expertise and use it to create a successful business.

The first step in identifying your expertise is to review your past experiences. Do a deep dive into your past professional history, and ask yourself the following questions:

- What is unique to you and sets you apart from others in your field?

- What accomplishments are you most proud of from your professional history?

- Are there any moments or achievements in a specific role that made you shine?

- Have you faced any challenges in your career and overcome them skillfully?

- Are there any projects or initiatives you've led that had a significant impact?

You also need to consider your personal experiences, skills, talents, hobbies, and passions.

- What are you naturally good at, like you were born with superpowers?

- What do people constantly come to you for help with because you're just that amazing?

- What do others consider your secret weapon or special talent that makes them go "Wow!" in awe?

- What is your ultimate claim to fame that fuels envy and admiration in others?

But wait, there's more! Let's dive deeper into uncovering your extraordinary potential:

- What sparks joy and excitement in your heart?

- What sets your soul on fire and ignites your creative spark?

- What dreams have you been nurturing secretly within?

- What challenges have you conquered that have shaped you into who you are today?

The answers to these captivating inquiries will guide you toward unlocking your true potential and stepping into a world of fulfillment and accomplishment. Embrace the journey, and let your extraordinary qualities shine brightly!

For example, if you have experience in human resources, you may have skills in communication, recruitment, and training. These skills can be used to start a consulting business. If you enjoy cooking and love to try out new recipes, you could turn your hobby into a catering or meal prep business. If you have a talent for graphic design, you could start a freelance design business.

Another way to identify your skills is to take an online skills assessment test. There are many free online tests that can help you identify your skills and strengths. These tests can help you determine areas where you excel and areas where you may need to improve. Once you have identified your skills, you can use them to create a business idea that aligns with your interests and expertise.

By reviewing your past personal and professional experiences, hobbies, and talents, and taking a skills assessment test, you can uncover hidden talents and skills that can be used to create a profitable business. Once you have identified your skills, it's important to analyze them and find ways to use them to add value to people's lives. By doing so, you can create a business that aligns with your interests and expertise and helps you achieve your entrepreneurial dreams. Remember, starting a business may be challenging, but it can also be rewarding. So go ahead and identify your skills and start creating your own business success story!

There is one essential factor to consider before starting down the entrepreneurial path—your emotions.

Starting a business is often considered a dream worth pursuing. However, the reality is, it's no walk in the park. Many aspiring entrepreneurs are clueless about navigating the treacherous path strewn with pitfalls. They meticulously plan, analyze market trends, research competition, and prepare for the grand launch. Yet, amidst all the chaos, one crucial element often goes overlooked—the power of emotions.

Building a business is more than just seizing an opportunity; it's about wholeheartedly embracing passion and conviction. Let's unravel the profound impact of emotions on business triumphs and explore why disregarding joy and succumbing to stress can lead entrepreneurs down the road to failure. Brace yourself for some enlightening revelations ahead!

Let's start this exciting journey by delving into the emotional aspect. Take a moment to ponder:

- What drives you to embark on this adventure?

- Is it to accomplish your dreams?

- Are you chasing your passions,

- or trying to boost your bank account?

It's crucial to consider your needs, desires, and aspirations. Grab a pen and jot down everything you hope to achieve and everything you want to steer clear of. Reflect upon what truly brings you joy and what doesn't. Envision the rewards and benefits you wish to shape your business around, whether it's the freedom to pick up your kids from school every day or the convenience of working from your cozy home. Make sure to consider which type of work makes you happy, too. You will spend a lot of time working on your business, so make it something you enjoy doing. Visualize your perfect experience as a business owner and build the business that aligns with your desires.

Make no mistake, it won't happen magically. The power is in your hands to craft the right business for you. Don't fall into the same trap as other entrepreneurs who make costly mistakes. They pick a cookie-cutter business that does not align with their emotions, and they dedicate their time and energy to building a business only to realize they don't actually enjoy what they've created. As a result, they miss out on the rewards they desire, finding themselves working longer hours for lesser returns. They fail to experience the fulfilling moments they initially sought, such as quality time with their family or the freedom to pursue their own passions. Let's learn from their missteps and discover a smarter, more rewarding path to entrepreneurial success.

When it comes to choosing a business, the bottom line is what really matters.

Launching a thriving business takes more than just money. It demands a profound grasp of the market, forging strategic alliances, out-of-the-box problem-solving, keen money management skills, and a penchant for learning from missteps. But perhaps above all, it hinges on valuing profits and constructing sustainable business frameworks. Because let's face it: You are trying to start a business, not develop an expensive hobby. So, let's not undervalue the potential in comprehending your earning prospects and mapping out a pathway to financial triumph. By meticulously strategizing and actualizing your entrepreneurial aspirations, you can pave the road for a lucrative and gratifying journey.

So, how do you pave the road to success? Creating a lucrative business requires more than just luck—it takes a comprehensive plan that maximizes your earnings. By diving into the market, identifying potential opportunities, and setting clear financial goals, you'll set your business up for success. Let's get real, you're in this to make serious cash. Why settle for anything less? So buckle up, and let's unlock your earning potential, turning your dream of a sustainable and profitable business into a reality.

In order to maximize profits, you will need to research the market to see what people want and what they are willing to pay for what you have to offer.

- What problem are you solving for your ideal customers?

- How are they currently solving that problem?

- How does your solution compare to the competition and what they offer?

- How can you do better than the competition at solving this problem?

You can learn the answers to these questions and get insights from customers about the problem you are solving, the solution competitors are offering, and what customers truly desire. You can uncover the strategies to outshine them, and you'll be able to tailor your offerings to exceed customer expectations. Uncover the secrets to providing a superior solution and seize the opportunity to impress. This distinctive approach will pave your path to success.

Many aspiring entrepreneurs reach this point and find themselves unsure of the next steps. This is a common challenge because crafting an offer is no easy task. My recommendation? Find someone who is successfully doing what you want to do, let their achievements inspire you, and adopt a similar framework. Once you've created your irresistible offer, it's showtime!

You have to roll up your sleeves and hit the ground running. Sell your offer with gusto. Don't forget to gather feedback along the way to refine and enhance your approach. This will ensure that you meet the needs of your customers and attract the right audience to make those sales and achieve the success you desire. Let's make magic happen!

Success is not a mere stroke of luck; it requires expertise,
emotional intelligence, and the drive to maximize your earnings.

Starting a business from scratch is no small feat. While I can't cover everything in just one chapter, I can provide some crucial advice. Before launching, it's vital to establish processes, policies, documentation, and a solid framework as the bedrock of your business. Neglecting these steps can lead to utter chaos once you enter the market, and trust me, I've witnessed it happen one too many times. Customer service is the secret sauce, so buckle up to handle the workload and deliver exceptional service.

From the moment we enter this world, we are an empty canvas, brimming with hope and infinite possibilities. But as life unfolds, doubts start to creep in, and confidence begins to waver. Fear of failure grabs hold, and the path to greatness remains uncharted territory. Too many souls trudge through life, never daring to believe in themselves. Yet the gravest mistake lies in leaving your dreams to chance. The haunting regret of "what if" looms larger than any failure. Breaking free from the cycle of self-doubt is no easy task, but trust me, it's a journey worth embarking on. Take that daring leap of faith and unlock limitless achievements you never thought possible. Don't let uncertainty hold you back. Trust in God's plan for your life, embrace the challenges, grow into the person he intended you to be, and watch yourself soar to extraordinary heights.

Elizabeth Corey

Founder of Vibrant Elephant Mindset
Confidence Coach Yogi

https://www.linkedin.com/in/vemconfidencecoach
https://www.facebook.com/Lizz.ConfidenceCoach/
https://www.instagram.com/biohack.life_lizz/
www.Vemconfidencecoach.biz
https://to.uptime.app/52ZtPtN9FGb

As the founder of Vibrant Elephant Mindset, a Confidence Coaching Program for entrepreneurial women. Here my mission or simply life purpose is to hold the light; the namaste philosophy. Behind that is where I built my mission statement for Vibrant Elephant; here I am the guiding the light and serving women who are tired of choosing to be SELF and work to find more flexible, confident VOICE in their business while being more present and happy within. My coaching program is tailored for each client and her lived experience and educational background that has led to this journey. I truly believe, "It does not matter how many times you fail, only how many times you get back up!" Enough on the business side, Lastly, there needs to be more play, rejuvenation, and thrills in life and that comes from inner work and many must-takes!

DISCOVERING MY VOICE

By Elizabeth Corey

Introduction

Hello, I'm Elizabeth Corey, but you might know me better as Lizz. If life were a book, mine would be a tapestry woven from threads of resilience, a narrative colored by challenges transformed into triumphs. From a tumultuous childhood navigating the stormy seas of foster care to standing today as the founder of the VOICE Confidence Coaching Program, my path has been anything but ordinary.

This book is more than just a collection of experiences; it's a beacon for those who feel that their voice has been muted by the cacophony of life's trials. It's for the entrepreneurial woman who stands on the precipice of her potential, seeking the courage to leap. Through the VOICE framework—Voice, Outward, Internal, Center, and Effectiveness—I offer not just insights but tools to liberate yourself from the mental shackles that bind you and step boldly into your power.

The Genesis of a Journey

My story begins in the fragmented world of foster care, a realm where stability was a foreign concept and the notion of a "home" was as fleeting as the wind. Voiceless and powerless, I was a ship without a rudder, tossed about at the whims of a system that I neither understood nor controlled. As a young girl, I quickly learned that to survive was to adapt, to blend into the backgrounds of various homes that never quite felt like my own.

Yet, amidst this chaos, there was a flicker of something more—a stubborn spark of resilience that refused to be extinguished. It was this resilience that carried me through the darkest moments, from the depths of addiction to the shadows of self-doubt that clung tightly to my psyche. Overcoming addiction wasn't just about reclaiming my health; it was about reclaiming my identity, stripping away the layers of who I was told to be to uncover who I truly am.

The Awakening of Voice

The concept of "voice" extends far beyond the mere act of speaking. It's about finding resonance with your authentic self; it's about the courage to express that self in a world that often urges conformity. For years, my voice was a mere whisper, lost in the cacophony of expectations and past traumas. It took decades for me to understand that the most profound strength lies in vulnerability, in the willingness to let your true self be seen and heard.

The corruption inside me brought pain and physical aches to my entire self, not only my psyche; later, through personal development, I discovered that these elements were self-induced—we give ourselves these pains. Pause for a moment. Think about how the general majority of babies are born without pain. It is from the corrupted self-will that pain occurs; at least, this is my story and teaching.

Let's give that pain a description. We can call it a "bug" that bites, and once it does, it implants something. What is that something? The bug bites us and implants an **"idea"** *to have our way of* **"freedom."** Stay with me because it took a very long time to settle, sink, and submerge into my subconscious that God's way was *bondage*. Yes, I know, just hit you with the capital G word, and if it's not for you, remove it and replace it with Universe, Source Power, Nature, Creation—anything that is larger than you—and let this resonate. When this *bug bites* it leads to fears and complexes; life turns on itself, never unfolding the way you want or I wanted, hence feeling stunted or in a rut.

My pivotal moment came unexpectedly during a routine team meeting in my late twenties. Tasked with presenting a project idea I believed in passionately, I anticipated resistance. Instead, I was met with support. That day, I learned that a clear, confident voice could not only open doors but could change the dynamics of a room. It was not just about being heard; it was about being understood and respected.

Dr. Gordon Allport says, "Paradoxically, 'self-expression' requires the capacity to lose oneself in the pursuit of objectives not primarily to the self." This was true for me up until that meeting, lost in the objectives of how life *should* look to standards not my own, based on what society or others projected onto me. "Should" is a foolish word; it is "would and could" smeared in humiliation when broken down. Standing in that meeting (real estate in timeshare sales), my inner voice broke free. The driving urge, the bug bite, was lost to a higher calling and I was found again in self-expression.

Standing in this meeting, sharing on a topic that passionately resonated in my soul, I realized that my career path was way off course and that this was a turning point in my life. The value of self-expression was vulnerability for the first time ever in my life. Again, a word that I personally defined as shameful, and my body was freely expressing it; later I would discover that this was Spirit-expression. Spirit-expression is when the body does without notice what the conscious mind and subconscious mind want it to do. Self-Expression and Spirit-Expression are where the subconscious and the conscious mind have one control of the Spirit and one single output, and that's harmony!

Affirmation: Today, no inhibitions, no fears, no complaints; only personal compliments, no suppression. Let in the power of total surrender.

Transforming Challenges into Triumphs

This realization marked the beginning of a transformation that reshaped every facet of my life. Embracing my voice allowed me to forge deeper connections, to turn superficial interactions into meaningful dialogues. Professionally, it catalyzed my journey from a background player to a leader and, ultimately, an advocate for others whose voices are still searching for their strength.

But finding my voice was only the first step. The true challenge lay in aligning this voice with my outward actions, in ensuring that the persona I presented to the world reflected the reality of who I was inside. This alignment did not happen overnight. It was a meticulous process of introspection, healing, and, most importantly, unlearning the destructive narratives that had governed my life.

The VOICE Framework

The VOICE framework is the distillation of all these lessons, a holistic approach to personal and professional empowerment. Each element—Voice, Outward, Internal, Center, and Effectiveness—serves as a pillar upon which a balanced and authentic life can be built.

- **Voice** is about discovering and honing your unique perspective, learning to articulate it with clarity and confidence.

- **Outward** focuses on how you present yourself to the world, ensuring that your external expressions align with your inner truth.

- **Internal** involves the introspective journey to confront and conquer the inner conflicts that threaten your peace.

- **Center** is about finding your equilibrium amidst life's chaos, maintaining your core stability no matter what storms may rage.

- **Effectiveness** measures the impact of aligning your voice with your actions, enhancing not only personal fulfillment but also your ability to inspire and lead others.

Why This Matters

As you turn the pages of this book, you will find both a mirror and a map. The mirror reflects not only my journey but also the potential that lies within each of us to transform our challenges into stepping stones. The map is the VOICE framework, a guide to navigating the complexities of personal and professional growth.

This chapter is for every woman who has ever doubted her worth, for every man who seeks to understand the challenges unique to the women in their lives, and for anyone who believes in the transformative power of finding and using one's voice. It's a testament to the fact that it's not just about surviving the storm—it's about learning to dance in the rain.

Together, let's embark on this journey of discovery and transformation. Let's find our voices, let's shout our truths from the rooftops, and let's turn our whispers into roars that echo far and wide.

V: Voice – Discovering and Scaling Your True Self

Introduction to Voice

In the landscape of personal and professional growth, "Voice" represents more than just the ability to speak out; it's about discovering and honing your true self and learning to express it authentically in every aspect of your life. My journey to finding my voice was not just about overcoming the silence imposed by my circumstances but about transforming that voice into a powerful tool for leadership and empowerment.

The Story of Discovering My Voice

Growing up in the disjointed world of foster care, I learned early on that being heard was a privilege I seldom enjoyed. My opinions and desires were often overshadowed by the immediate needs of survival and adaptation. This environment taught me to mute my own voice, to suppress my true thoughts and feelings to fit into the transient homes and schools that dotted my childhood.

As I ventured into the professional world, this pattern of silence followed. Early in my career, I found myself hesitating to speak up in meetings or to present my ideas, plagued by the deep-seated fear that my thoughts were not valuable. This all changed during a pivotal meeting in my late twenties—a routine presentation that unexpectedly became the turning point of my life and career. I presented a controversial project idea, expecting resistance, and was met instead with enthusiastic support. This experience was a revelation—it taught me that having a voice and using it effectively could reshape my reality.

I highly recommend that you pause here and let the bug-bite metaphor sink in, getting comfortable with the variation of higher Will that you can surrender to. Finding and honing my voice was not a liability; instead, it was an asset, and that corrupted fear was self-will run riot. In spite of a controversial idea that was stunting the trajectory of the growth of the company, co-workers, and myself, once again that inner voice bravely stood up and shone with courage. Here was the first lesson of vulnerability meeting humility in terms of standing for what was right in the eye of humanity and not profit; again, the lesson of Spirit-Expression.

Scaling Your Voice

Once I recognized the power of my voice, the next challenge was to scale this newfound capability, to extend its reach and influence. Here are the steps I took that you, too, can follow in order to scale your voice in both personal and professional realms:

Self-Reflection: Start with introspection. Understand what makes you unique. Identify your core beliefs, values, and the experiences that shape your perspective. For me, journaling and meditation were instrumental in this process.

Skill Development: Enhance your communication skills through public speaking courses, writing workshops, or leadership training. I took every opportunity to speak publicly, from small team meetings to larger industry conferences, refining my ability to articulate my thoughts clearly and compellingly.

Feedback and Adaptation: Embrace feedback on your communication style. I regularly sought input from trusted mentors and peers, which helped me fine-tune my approach and ensure that my voice not only was heard but also resonated with my audience.

Visibility: Increase your visibility by contributing to platforms that align with your values and expertise. Write articles, participate in podcasts, or speak at public events. Each of these activities helps amplify your voice beyond your immediate circle.

Network and Connect: Build a network of supporters and collaborators who share your vision or complement your goals. Networking has been crucial to expanding my influence, providing me with platforms I could not have accessed on my own.

Mentorship: As you grow, offer mentorship to others. Teaching is a powerful way to solidify your own knowledge and to give back, helping others find and use their voices. This not only scales your impact but also strengthens your leadership presence.

Sustainability: Finally, ensure the sustainability of your voice by staying true to your core message and continuously evolving as you gain more experiences and insights. This means revisiting and possibly revising your foundational beliefs as you grow and learn.

Stories of Impact

Let me share a quick story about Sarah, one of my coaching clients. Sarah was a mid-level manager who struggled with public speaking due to her introverted nature. Through our work together, focusing on the steps outlined above, she not only overcame her fear but also learned to use her voice as a powerful tool for leadership. She eventually led a successful campaign for gender equity in her company, which started with her ability to articulate a compelling vision and rally others around her cause.

Another example is from a workshop I conducted on effective communication. One participant, Mike, learned to reshape his approach to team meetings. Instead of dominating conversations, he learned to listen actively and encourage others to contribute, effectively amplifying not just his own voice but also the voices of his team members. This shift dramatically improved his team's performance and morale.

Action Steps

To scale your voice effectively, consider these actionable steps:

Assess Your Current State: Evaluate how effectively you are currently using your voice. Are you speaking up? Are you being heard?

Set Specific Goals: What do you want to achieve by scaling your voice? Is it leadership within your workplace, influence within your community, or something else?

Develop a Plan: Based on your goals, develop a strategic plan to enhance and scale your voice. Include specific actions, resources needed, and timelines.

Implement and Iterate: Put your plan into action. Remember, this is a dynamic process. Be prepared to iterate on your strategy as you learn what works and what doesn't.

Measure Your Impact: Finally, find ways to measure the impact of your voice. This could be through the feedback you receive, the opportunities that come your way, or the tangible outcomes of your initiatives.

Finding and scaling your voice is not merely about personal empowerment; it's about creating ripples that can transform the fabric of your community and beyond. As you embark on this journey, remember that each step forward not only amplifies your own voice but can also light the way for others. Let's raise our voices together, not just to speak, but to resonate and inspire.

O: Outward – Expressing Your Authentic Self

Introduction to Outward Expression

Outward expression is the visible manifestation of your inner voice. It's how you present yourself to the world, how you communicate your values, and how you act on your beliefs. On my journey, learning to express myself authentically was both challenging and transformative. It required not just understanding who I was but also having the courage to unapologetically show that person to the world.

The Story of Overcoming External Challenges

My early days of outward expression were fraught with challenges. Coming from a background where I was often silenced or overlooked, I initially found it difficult to assert myself in spaces where voices like mine were rarely heard. I remember one particular instance early in my career when I felt that my ideas were being dismissed not on their merit but simply because of who I was—a young woman trying to make her mark in a male-dominated industry. This experience was disheartening, but it was also a turning point. It ignited a fierce determination in me to not only be heard but to ensure that others were heard as well.

The real test came when I launched my own business. Suddenly, it wasn't just about expressing my ideas within a company; it was about presenting my vision to the world. Building my brand and establishing my website, <u>VEM Confidence Coach</u>, became central to this effort. My website wasn't just a digital space—it was a platform where I could articulate my mission, showcase my services, and share client successes. It became a tool for connecting with like-minded individuals and attracting clients who resonated with my message.

Scaling Your Outward Expression

Here's how I scaled my outward expression and how you can do the same:

Branding: Develop a personal or business brand that reflects your true self. Use your website, social media, and all public communications to consistently convey your core messages. Make sure these platforms highlight what you stand for.

Public Speaking: Embrace opportunities to speak publicly, whether at conferences, workshops, or online webinars. Each platform offers a chance to refine your message and reach a broader audience.

Content Creation: Create and share content that aligns with your values. Blogs, podcasts, and videos are powerful tools for expressing your perspectives and engaging with a community.

Community Engagement: Actively participate in or create communities that reflect your values. Engaging with these groups not only strengthens your voice but also amplifies it through collective action.

Feedback Loop: Establish a system for gathering feedback on your outward expressions. Use this input to adjust and enhance how you communicate and present yourself.

Personal Story of Impact

During the early stages of my website, I shared a blog post about overcoming fear in business. The response was overwhelming. People from all over the world reached out to share their stories and thank me for the inspiration. This feedback showed me the power of authentic expression and reinforced the importance of sharing our true selves.

Client Story of Transformation

One of my clients, Maria, struggled with public speaking due to a fear of being judged. Through our sessions, she learned to align her outward expressions with her inner values. Maria's breakthrough came during a large conference when she delivered a compelling talk on women's leadership, which was met with resounding applause and numerous invitations for future speaking engagements. Her success story, featured on my website, has inspired countless other women to embrace their voices and express themselves boldly.

Action Steps

To enhance your outward expression, consider these actionable steps:

Audit Your Current Expression: Review your current public presence, including social media, website, and any public communications. Does it accurately reflect your inner voice?

Set Clear Objectives: Define what you want to achieve through your outward expression. Is it to influence, to inspire, to educate, or to build a community?

Develop a Strategy: Based on your objectives, craft a strategy for how you will enhance your outward expression. Decide on the platforms, types of content, and key messages you will use.

Implement Your Plan: Start putting your strategy into action. Update your website, start that blog, or begin that speaking tour. Remember, consistency is key.

Measure and Adjust: Finally, set up metrics to measure the impact of your outward expressions. Monitor engagement and feedback, and be prepared to adjust your approach to better align with your objectives.

Expressing your authentic self outwardly is not just about being seen; it's about being recognized for who you truly are and what you stand for. As we navigate through our professional and personal lives, let's strive to present ourselves authentically, creating spaces in which our true voices are not only heard but also celebrated. Let's transform our outward expression into a beacon for change and a call to action for others to join us in this journey of authentic living.

I: Internal – Aligning Your Inner World

Introduction to Internal Alignment

The journey to internal alignment is perhaps the most personal and profound aspect of the VOICE framework. It's about reconciling your external actions with your inner truths, ensuring that what the world sees is a reflection of your authentic self. For me, this journey has involved deep introspection facilitated by yoga, overcoming addiction, and regular meditation—each serving as a critical pathway to understanding and harmonizing my internal landscape.

The Role of Yoga in Internal Alignment

Yoga came into my life as a physical practice, but quickly revealed its mental and spiritual depths. Through each pose, each breath, I learned to quiet the noise of the world and listen to my inner voice. The mat became a place of discovery, where I could explore the tensions and traumas held in my body and begin to release them. Yoga taught me about presence and how to live in the moment, lessons that proved invaluable as I worked to align my internal world.

Overcoming Addiction

Addiction was a formidable barrier on my path to internal alignment. It masked my true feelings and needs, creating a fog around my internal compass. Breaking free from addiction wasn't just about ceasing a harmful habit; it was about uncovering the deeper issues that led me to seek solace in substances. Recovery introduced me to the power of vulnerability and the importance of facing my fears and pains rather than numbing them. This part of my journey was critical, as it allowed me to begin the real work of alignment—understanding and addressing the root causes of my unrest.

Embracing Meditation

Meditation complimented my yoga practice by providing a structured way to delve into the quiet spaces of my mind. It helped me cultivate a state of observation without judgment, allowing me to recognize and redirect harmful patterns of thought. The practice of meditation brought clarity and calm, which were essential for sustaining the mental energy needed to maintain my sobriety and continue my journey toward alignment.

Journey to Alignment

Aligning my internal world has been a multifaceted process. It began by acknowledging the discrepancies between my actions and my true feelings—recognizing where I was performing rather than being genuine. Yoga, with its introspective and restorative nature, was instrumental in this phase, teaching me how to listen to my body and, by extension, my inner self.

As I moved deeper into recovery from addiction, I engaged more profoundly with therapy and support groups, where I learned the tools to dismantle the façade I had built around my life. These tools included open communication, continuous self-assessment, and the regular practice of self-forgiveness, which were crucial for realigning my actions with my values.

Meditation deepened this alignment by helping me develop greater self-awareness and control over my responses to external pressures. It allowed me to approach situations with a clear mind, reducing impulsive reactions and increasing thoughtful responses that reflect my true intentions.

Client Story of Transformation

One of my clients, Jenna, embarked on a similar path. Struggling with high stress and low self-esteem, she found solace in yoga and meditation, which we incorporated into her personalized coaching program. Through these practices, Jenna learned to recognize her intrinsic worth and gradually aligned her daily activities with her core values. Her transformation was profound—she not only achieved a significant promotion at work but also became a more present and engaged parent and partner.

Action Steps

If you're seeking internal alignment, consider these actionable steps:

Engage in Mindfulness Practices: Start a regular practice of yoga and meditation. These disciplines can help you connect with your inner self and provide clarity.

Seek Professional Help: If you're dealing with issues like addiction, don't hesitate to seek professional help. Therapists, counselors, and support groups can offer guidance and support on your journey.

Journal Regularly: Keep a journal of your thoughts, feelings, and discoveries. Writing can be a powerful tool for reflection and can help you track your progress toward alignment.

Set Aside Time for Self-Reflection: Dedicate regular periods to self-reflection. Use this time to assess your feelings, thoughts, and behaviors, and consider whether they align with your true self.

Practice Self-Forgiveness: Learn to forgive yourself for past actions that don't align with your current values. Understanding that change is a process can help you move forward without the burden of past missteps.

The journey to internal alignment is ongoing and deeply personal. It requires patience, persistence, and the willingness to delve into the depths of your own psyche. As you embark on this journey, remember that each step brings you closer to a life lived with authenticity and peace. Embrace the tools and practices that resonate with you, and allow them to guide you to a place of profound inner harmony.

C: Center – Finding Balance Between Strengths and Weaknesses

Introduction to Center

In the quest for personal and professional fulfillment, finding your center involves striking a delicate balance between leveraging your strengths and addressing your weaknesses. This balance, critical yet challenging to achieve, is the fulcrum upon which personal growth and professional success pivot. It's about understanding where you naturally excel and where you might need to put in extra effort to overcome challenges.

The Importance of Leveraging Strengths

My journey has taught me that focusing on your strengths is not just about playing to your advantages; it's about maximizing your potential in the places you're already poised to succeed. For me, the ability to empathize deeply with others and connect on a personal level has always been a natural strength. This skill has been the cornerstone of my coaching career, enabling me to reach into the hearts of my clients and truly understand their struggles and aspirations.

In every coaching session, I bring this strength to the forefront, creating a safe and understanding environment where clients feel seen and heard. This ability to connect has not only empowered my clients but has also fueled my passion and enthusiasm for my work, making every success story a personal victory.

Addressing Weaknesses for Growth

While it's essential to build on your strengths, acknowledging and working on your weaknesses is equally important. Early in my career, I found myself grappling with issues of self-control and consistency. These were not merely minor hurdles; they were significant obstacles that threatened to derail my progress and limit my impact.

I tackled these weaknesses head-on, recognizing that without developing these areas, my ability to succeed and sustain my business long-term would be compromised. I committed to a rigorous schedule, set strict goals for personal discipline, and sought feedback to improve. This process was challenging and often uncomfortable, but it was necessary for growth.

Achieving Balance for Overall Improvement

Balance in personal development is about creating a harmonious approach that allows you to thrive while continually pushing your boundaries. It's not about being perfect in every aspect but about recognizing where you are strong and where you are not, and finding ways to bring these into alignment.

In my personal life, the strength of forming deep connections paved the way for launching my coaching business. However, turning this talent into a successful enterprise required me to hone other skills, particularly in areas where I was less confident, like public speaking and consistent daily operations.

The Journey of Public Speaking

Public speaking was once my greatest vulnerability—an activity I would avoid at all costs. However, recognizing that this skill was essential for spreading my message and growing my audience, I began to face this challenge head-on. I started small, speaking at local events and gathering feedback from every appearance. Gradually, as I applied the lessons learned and practiced relentlessly, my confidence grew.

This growth did not happen overnight. It was the result of many small steps, each one building on the last, until public speaking transformed from a weakness into one of my most effective tools for connecting with a broader audience. Now, I use public speaking not just as a method of communication but as a platform for inspiring change and motivating others.

Implementing a Balanced Strategy

Self-Assessment: Regularly evaluate your strengths and weaknesses. Be honest and objective about where you excel and where you require improvement.

Goal Setting: Set specific, measurable goals for both leveraging your strengths and addressing your weaknesses. Ensure these goals are challenging yet achievable.

Skill Development: Invest in training and development opportunities. For strengths, seek advanced courses that challenge you further. For weaknesses, start with foundational courses that build competence.

Feedback Mechanisms: Create systems to receive continuous feedback. This could be through mentors, peers, or even client reviews. Use this feedback to adjust your strategies and improve.

Daily Practice: Incorporate practice into your daily routine. Whether it's honing a strength or improving a weakness, consistent action is key to making progress.

Reflection and Adjustment: Reflect on your progress regularly. What's working? What's not? Be prepared to pivot your strategies to better align with your goals.

Finding your center is not about achieving a perfect balance but about navigating the complexities of your personal and professional life in a way that maximizes your potential. By understanding and embracing both your strengths and your weaknesses, you can create a more fulfilling and impactful journey.

As we strive to find our center, let us remember that the journey is as important as the destination. It is through the process of balancing, adjusting, and aligning that we truly discover our capabilities and our potential. Let this knowledge guide you as you continue to evolve and grow, making each step an opportunity to learn and improve. Embrace the challenge, for it is in the challenge that we find our true strength.

E: Effectiveness – Harnessing Your Strengths as a Woman Entrepreneur

Introduction to Effectiveness

In the VOICE framework, "Effectiveness" encapsulates the tangible outcomes of aligning your voice, outward expression, and internal harmony to achieve professional and personal success. For women entrepreneurs, this often means navigating a complex landscape of societal expectations, personal commitments, and the intrinsic challenges of business leadership. In this section, we explore how to enhance effectiveness by leveraging unique strengths, managing challenges like ADHD, and implementing strategic actions to find our place and make a mark on the world.

The Entrepreneurial Journey and Its Challenges

My own journey into entrepreneurship was anything but straightforward. Starting as a woman in the competitive world of business coaching, I had to carve out a space in which I could not only exist but thrive. This required a deep understanding of my unique strengths—empathy, resilience, and a knack for connecting with people on a personal level. However, it also meant confronting and overcoming the inherent challenges of being a woman in business, such as battling stereotypes and breaking through industry barriers.

Furthermore, managing ADHD as an adult added another layer of complexity to this process. ADHD can make it challenging to maintain focus, organize tasks, and manage time effectively—skills that are critical in business. Overcoming these hurdles was essential to not only establishing my business but to ensuring its ongoing success and growth.

Leveraging Strengths in Business

Focusing on my strengths has always been my strategy for enhancing effectiveness. By channeling my ability to empathize with clients and connect genuinely, I was able to build a coaching business that truly resonates with women entrepreneurs. This approach not only set me apart from competitors but also built a loyal client base that valued the personal touch I brought to my coaching sessions.

One significant story that comes to mind is from early in my business. I was working with a client, Sarah, who struggled to balance her start-up ambitions with raising a young family. By focusing on what I do best—providing empathetic, tailored coaching—I helped Sarah implement systems that maximized her strengths in vision and creativity while outsourcing tasks in areas where she felt less competent. This strategy not only helped her business grow but also allowed her to find a better balance between her professional and personal life.

Addressing Weaknesses and Implementing Solutions

While leveraging strengths is crucial, addressing weaknesses is equally important. For me, managing ADHD meant finding innovative ways to handle multitasking and maintain productivity. I adopted tools and techniques such as time-blocking and priority setting, which were game-changers in managing my daily tasks and long-term projects.

Additionally, I recognized early on that public speaking was a critical skill I needed to develop to expand my influence and reach more people. I started small, seeking opportunities to speak at local business events and gradually working my way up to larger conferences. With each experience, I gathered feedback, honed my skills, and grew more comfortable in this role.

Action Plan for Enhancing Effectiveness

For women entrepreneurs looking to enhance their effectiveness, here's a structured action plan:

Identify and Leverage Strengths: Take stock of your unique strengths and consider how they can be applied to overcome business challenges. Utilize tools like strength assessments or feedback from peers to gain insights.

Identify and Develop Weak Areas: Identify areas in which you lack skills or confidence and develop a plan for improvement. This might include training, mentoring, or partnering with others who complement your skills.

Implement Organizational Tools: For managing ADHD or simply staying on top of business demands, incorporate organizational tools such as digital planners, apps for task management, and methods like the Pomodoro Technique to improve focus and productivity.

Expand Your Network: Build and engage with a network of like-minded entrepreneurs. Networking can provide support, insights, and opportunities that can propel your business forward.

Seek Feedback and Iterate: Regularly seek feedback on your business operations and personal performance. Use this feedback to make informed adjustments and continuously improve your effectiveness.

Prioritize Self-Care: Managing a business requires energy and resilience. Ensure you are supporting your mental and physical health through regular exercise, adequate rest, and hobbies that rejuvenate you.

Set Measurable Goals: Define clear, measurable goals for both business outcomes and personal development. Regularly review these goals to track progress and make necessary adjustments.

Effectiveness as a woman entrepreneur isn't just about achieving business success; it's about creating a sustainable model that supports your overall well-being and life goals. It requires a balanced approach that acknowledges both your strengths and areas for improvement. By taking strategic actions tailored to your unique situation, you can enhance your effectiveness, overcome challenges, and achieve both your personal and professional aspirations.

In the end, remember that the journey of entrepreneurship is a marathon, not a sprint. Each step you take builds on the last, propelling you forward toward success and fulfillment. As you continue to navigate this path, keep your values at the center, use your intuition and Self-Expression, and keep it centered for the Spirit-Expression.

Empowering Your Journey Forward

As we close this chapter on navigating the VOICE framework—Voice, Outward, Internal, Center, and Effectiveness—I hope that the stories shared and strategies outlined have resonated with you, illuminating paths not only for personal triumph but also for fostering deeper connections with others. Throughout, we've delved into topics seldom discussed openly, embracing vulnerability not as a weakness but as a core strength. It's through this vulnerability that we connect most authentically with others, and it's where true growth begins.

Empowering Women Like Us

Whether you're overcoming personal struggles, setting out on your entrepreneurial journey, or simply looking to find balance in a demanding world, know that you are not alone. Many women share these challenges, and it's for each one of us that this chapter was written. Here's a concise plan to help you harness the lessons learned and apply them to your life:

Reflect on Your VOICE: Take the time to reflect on each aspect of the VOICE framework. Identify areas where you feel strong and aspects where you may need support. Self-awareness is the first step toward meaningful change.

Set Concrete Goals: Based on your reflection, set specific, achievable goals. Whether it's improving your public speaking skills, enhancing your business acumen, or finding peace through meditation, define what success looks like for you in each area.

Seek Support and Community: You don't have to walk this path alone. Engage with communities of like-minded individuals who can offer support, guidance, and encouragement. Whether it's joining local networking groups, finding online communities, or participating in workshops, surround yourself with people who uplift and inspire you.

Commit to Continuous Learning: Dedicate yourself to lifelong learning and growth. This might mean reading books, attending seminars, or pursuing further education. Each step in learning is a step toward a more empowered self.

Practice Self-Compassion and Patience: Change doesn't happen overnight. Be patient with yourself and practice self-compassion. Celebrate your victories, no matter how small, and learn from the challenges without harsh judgment.

Book a Free Coaching Session

For those who see themselves in the stories shared or who resonate with the struggles and successes discussed, I invite you to book a free coaching session with me. It's a safe space to explore your goals, challenges, and dreams. Together, we can map out a path to your success, leveraging the VOICE framework to create a life and career filled with purpose and passion. To schedule your session, please visit Book a Session on my website.

The Power of Vulnerability

In writing this chapter, a great deal of what has been mentioned is enveloped in vulnerability. This vulnerability is the bedrock of authenticity and resilience. In our society, these topics are often skirted around, deemed too sensitive or private to be discussed openly. However, embracing our vulnerabilities can lead to a profound strength that is unmatched, allowing us to connect with others on a deeper level and grow beyond our perceived limits.

Moving Forward

As you move forward, remember that the journey to finding and using your voice, expressing yourself authentically, aligning your internal beliefs with your external actions, finding your center, and enhancing your effectiveness is ongoing. It evolves as you evolve. The VOICE framework is not just a tool for personal and professional development—it's a guide for living a life that is true to your deepest values and aspirations.

Let this chapter be the start of your journey, not the end. Continue to explore, to question, and to grow. And most importantly, allow yourself to be vulnerable, for it is in those moments that we are most open to the possibilities of what we can become. Together, let's redefine vulnerability, turning it into a stepping stone for empowerment and success.

Focus your attention on the linguistic choices you make with yourself first and foremost before others; this is a massive encouragement! Inside this chapter, I shared a few examples of times I had to identify and redefine, for they shaped the reality that was my existence: should, vulnerability, and humility. Not to mention wants, needs, success, strength, character, money, and control. These lay the foundation for what we as humans build our standards, views, and mindset around.

Life is glowing with life; the decision is ultimately yourself for the making and creating yet still we harness this ability to manage to dull the greatness inside the glowing light. Let this be your opportunity to glow, radiate, shine brighter than the sun or stars, and show the world and others simply how perfectly imperfect your unique voice truly is.

Love & Confidence,
Lizz

Edwina Adams

Founder of Let's Make Some Noise

https://www.linkedin.com/in/edwinaadams
https://www.facebook.com/groups/letsmakesomenoiseprivategroup
https://www.instagram.com/official_edwinaadams
http://edwinaadams.com
https://youtube.com/@letsmakesomenoisepodcast

Edwina Adams is resilient with a diverse background. She is a military veteran and a retired paramedic and she has nearly two decades of entrepreneurial experience. Edwina is a loyal friend, loving wife, and mom who adores cool shoes.

Edwina not only survived challenging situations, including her first marriage to a con man, a near-death experience, founding a business that was one of the first of its kind in America, and becoming an industry leader with multiple industry e-books, but she emerged as a source of encouragement for others facing adversity.

Now, Edwina dedicates her life to helping others know they too can overcome obstacles and thrive in life. She teaches that adversity is your greatest asset, drawing upon her journey of survival and empowerment. Edwina is on a mission to motivate others to make NOISE which is her acronym for a Narrative Of Inspiration, Strength, and Encouragement.

BECOME A NOISE-MAKER: TURN YOUR ADVERSITY INTO A NARRATIVE OF INSPIRATION, STRENGTH, AND ENCOURAGEMENT

By Edwina Adams

Sometimes, as a woman, you feel like your dreams will be the last ones to come to fruition, especially if you have family commitments like a husband, kids, or aging parents. The pressure to prioritize others over ourselves can deter us from pursuing our dreams, leading to a sense of disappointment and avoidance of dreaming altogether. Balancing caring for others with personal aspirations becomes difficult amidst persistent life challenges. Overcoming adversity is crucial for personal growth.

For all the phenomenal women reading this chapter, this is tailor-written for you—crafted with love, sprinkled with encouragement, and wrapped in the belief that we, as women, deserve a chorus of cheerleaders. I've been dubbed "Edwina the Encourager," a beacon of resilience in a world that has tried to derail my journey on multiple occasions. My life story resembles one of the quilts my grandmother made. Patched together with love and made from many different pieces of encouragement passed down through generations of a loving family. I'm thankful for my family, for sure. There may be a few blemishes on this quilt, that is my life, now but it's still unique and full of beauty.

Vocabulary.com defines the word *narrative* as "A story that you write or tell someone, usually in great detail." My narrative may become captivating to you because there were many times in my life when I was very discouraged. Being surrounded by love as a child, and despite being a middle child myself, the essence of my early years is warm and positive. Then I grew up! Life can drain you, am I right?

I want to share with you how turning your adversity into positive NOISE is a game changer. See, NOISE is my acronym for a Narrative

Of Inspiration, Strength, and Encouragement. And I believe your adversity is your greatest asset in crafting an incredible narrative. I began using what I call the ROCKY WATER approach to make NOISE no matter what adversity I was going through.

As "Edwina the Encourager," I'm here to do just that! To encourage you to be a NOISE-maker too! I'm not just nudging you to Dream Big; my goal is to inspire you to have your dreams take flight, even in the face of any adversity you may be dealing with now or if new adversity pops up in your life. Your journey and the challenges you face are important to making these dreams come true and will, more than likely, be distinctly different from the well-laid roads of our male counterparts. Many times, we women must be trailblazers instead of using those well-traveled paths made by the men doing similar things.

Let me set the record straight here, though. I'm not attempting to make this a men vs. women issue. I adore men. I was blessed to grow up with loving men in my life and know from experience that when a man steps into true manhood, they empower women to do great things. So no man-hating here. But ladies, we are spectacular, adorned with unique abilities and capacities that paint the world in vibrant hues. Own that, girl. Don't be afraid to be humble about it either. Humility will take you much further than boastfulness, and doing things with a chip on your shoulder will create negativity - you want to create NOISE.

Despite the unexpected detours that adulthood brought me, I was able to get back on track and have done so with an infectious attitude. But how did I navigate the seas of adversity, maintaining genuine optimism that wasn't just "toxic positivity?" And, most importantly, how can you do the same?

Here is what I believe. To thrive in life, one does not need to desire a lack of adversity; one chooses to embrace adversity and turn it into NOISE.

After my trials in life and business (including thriving after my divorce from an actual con man and later surviving a near-death experience), I now host a podcast called *Let's Make Some Noise*, where I share how I overcame those obstacles and encourage others to share their stories of adversity. I am also a motivational speaker and love to speak to women and audiences about this subject.

At the time of writing this book, I am currently dealing with heart failure for a second time with my heart only functioning at 18%. As I write, I'm wearing a defibrillating LifeVest™. I must wear the LifeVest™ because when your heart is functioning below 35%, you are at risk for sudden death due to the increased possibility of a lethal arrhythmia (heart rhythm). And I have to say, using my ROCKY WATER approach to life is not just a cute saying. I implement this in my life, and it's why I am currently creating positive NOISE every day even while experiencing heart failure. I'm so grateful to have this outlook on life, and I'm told daily that I am beaming with life even in the face of a health crisis and even though I'm not at my physical best. I want you to be resilient, regardless of life's challenges, too!

Before I explain what the ROCKY WATER approach is, I thought I'd share some of the adversities I have overcome. Perhaps you will identify with some of it or recognize something similar in your own life:

The Adversity of Balance:

A woman able to balance motherhood and a career is a lie. I've tried the balancing act; you probably have, too. It's exhausting, isn't it? And…you still feel like you are not doing anything right.

After 16 years of business ownership, I've learned this as a woman entrepreneur: The notion of a woman business owner, a working mom, or a stay-at-home mom with a dream of writing a book or building a dream and achieving what has been dubbed "work-life balance" is unrealistic and impractical in today's dynamic work environment. Instead, the focus should shift toward attaining a state of harmony between professional pursuits and personal responsibilities.

This perspective acknowledges the complex nature of women's lives, encompassing career ambitions, familial duties, and personal aspirations.

I urge you to strive for harmony instead of the elusive "balance." Continually striving for balance will most likely leave you feeling like a failure in both business and life—and that, my friend, is just not true.

You are NOT a failure!

If you are a woman who loves others well and has big dreams of her own, I hope you find the harmony needed to pursue both. As I already mentioned, your path to pursue your own business, a career, or a side gig while simultaneously taking care of your household most likely will not look anything like the path the men in your life take (trust me). And that's ok. We were made differently, and we have a powerful role in our families, but we were all made to love and to create, and with this desire will come new forms of adversity—how will you overcome it? If you quit striving for balance and focus on harmony, if a cancer scare pops up or the business loan you needed to keep your business afloat doesn't come through, you can more easily get through those trials and handle the adversity.

I encourage you to shift your mindset away from one of creating balance. Balance is the ability to maintain stability and control. In my experience, I have found that focusing on creating balance feels like living as if you are walking a tightrope. What happens if you fall off that tightrope? Failure, pain, death—nothing good. It's anxiety inducing. I lived like this for too many years and created my own anxiety living that way. While I'm not perfect, I have finally learned to have a mindset of creating harmony instead of balance. When I think of harmony, I think of different components coexisting and supporting each other in a sustainable way. If things are not harmonious, I don't feel like I'm losing my balance and about to fall; instead I feel like something could be better and I take time to see how I can get things to be harmonious, but it's less pressure on me than feeling like I must maintain control of everything. Have I convinced you that striving for harmony rather than balance is much less anxiety inducing? I hope so.

The Adversity of Your Dreams Not Taking Priority:

Have you ever been encouraged by someone or something, even a movie, then felt like you could accomplish something big? You get inspiration to start something, to build something, or even to write your own book, and then the reality hits that you have diapers to change, grocery shopping, and laundry for the family—all while you are already running out of steam. You think to yourself, "There is no way I have time to start or accomplish a dream—it's not the priority." This is where I feel that having a community can help. We are creatures that thrive when we have good community and connections. Within those communities and connections, when we get encouragement from others and give encouragement to others, we see growth in individuals that usually results in positivity for everyone. On the contrary, when someone is struggling with moving forward in their life due to feeling overwhelmed and alone, it can stop them from living out their dreams. It's also very common to have a great idea and then feel like the world is out to get you and stop you from ever accomplishing it. Have you experienced this? I know I sure have.

The Adversity of a Bad Marriage or Divorce:

I first got married at the age of twenty-four to a man seven years my senior, and that marriage lasted seven years. He turned out to be a con man who left me feeling very discouraged and confused. He also fooled some highly intelligent, well-trained people who had been his close friends. I tell you this so you can understand how good my ex was at fooling people. Even with that, it made me feel stupid, and I was full of shame, especially in front of those who, to this day, still don't know the full story (most don't). And believe me, people love to assume things about you when someone does you dirty. But this was a massive derailment in my life, and at the time, I didn't know what the next day would bring me or how I was supposed to navigate all the changes.

I finally began writing a book about my first marriage and am currently still working on it. I do know this: A version of me died with him and that relationship. I'll never allow him to be a part of my life again—he's been out of it since 2007—but I have forgiven him. That forgiveness is what released me from him completely. He isn't allowed to weigh me down with harbored anger anymore. My life is greater than his deception. I deserve to go on living a free, loving life, and I knew that wouldn't happen if I remained bitter about him and my past. I love the new version of me that emerged stronger, fiercer, and less afraid of what life may throw at me.

I'll admit, my resiliency is in big part due to my faith and personal relationship with God. I believe if there wasn't a spiritual side to life, then what my ex did to me and many others wouldn't have been perceived as wrong. If there is no spirit in us or a higher spirit (God), then what makes anything wrong? But our spirit knows when we are treated wrongly or being lied to. Even if we trick our brains into believing those things aren't happening to us, somehow our spirit knows.

After this forgiveness, I was able to open myself up to love again, and I even remarried. I am fortunate to have a supportive husband who embraces the new me and who created a family with me. Our son and daughter are a daily reminder of the rebirth that can happen with forgiveness and healing, and I'm grateful for a second chance at having a happy home.

The Adversity of Being a Woman in a Man's World:

A little more about me so you understand where I'm coming from: I predominately spent my life in male-dominated arenas. As a military veteran and a retired paramedic, I was surrounded by testosterone and different viewpoints than most women of the world. Even so, I was able to establish respect and gain leadership positions in these arenas, and I'm grateful for the experiences. Post-divorce, I waltzed into the entrepreneurial world, yet again shadowed by the towering figures of men. My mentors, bless their hearts, were men—stellar in their own right and full of wisdom, and I'm thankful for each of them. But they were a tad detached from the intricate dance of womanhood.

The Adversity of Motherhood:

I was a nearly 40-year-old mom to a four-month-old baby girl and a (barely) two-year-old, active little boy. They were both still in diapers and only 19 months apart. At this same time, my husband and I had recently sold a business we built together so he could go back to school full-time. I was supportive of him going back to school to pursue his dream of becoming a mental health therapist, but because I'd had another big dream of my own for seven years, I decided it was finally time to go for it. I created one of the first automated and eco-friendly trash can cleaning businesses in America. This was challenging because no one had ever heard of these services, and potential clients weren't looking for it. I was also a sleep-deprived zombie-mom with no money for a babysitter. My own family lived out of state, and I had a husband who was at school all day with homework to do in the evenings, AND now this new "infant" of a business was demanding more and more of my time if I wanted to grow it—which I did. I believed in it and didn't want to give up, but I was often angry because I couldn't get out and freely grow the business like I knew I should be doing to make it work. One day my husband said, "All this business does is make you angry; you need to get rid of it or change your attitude," and that…pissed me off!

But I kept thinking about what he'd said. He was right. I didn't want to be an angry mom, and that was all I had to give my kids, so I prayed hard. I said, "God, I don't want to give up but I need help." He gave me a feeling of peace, and it took some work on my part, but I was able to say to myself, "These babies won't be babies long; be their mom first and a businesswoman second." I knew in my heart that my business would grow; it would just have to grow much slower than I had planned and would grow much slower than my son and daughter. I still cared about and worked on the business, but I intentionally found mom groups, so I had regular meet-ups with other moms for my mental health and built-in play dates with other kids for my son and daughter. The business started growing organically, although slowly. I made a lot of mistakes and had to figure them out on my own since there weren't groups of people from that industry to learn from yet. Through my social media, I began to have men from nearly every state in America calling me, asking me what kind of business this was and how they could do it. Within a year and half, I spoke with over 200 men, sharing my knowledge freely and openly—telling them what not to do and what worked best and why, and the industry began to grow. I started an industry Facebook group to share knowledge with more people and learn from new companies that were beginning to pop up.

I had become an industry leader, but due to prioritizing my familial duties as a wife and stay-at-home mom, the men I had encouraged and taught best practices to were booming in their businesses, and many had wives who assisted them in their businesses while I had no one helping me. I was proud of them but felt like a failure—again. "Why did I think I could go for my dreams right now?" That was my thought.

As of writing this, I am just now entering my 10th year in the industry. I recently took on a new co-owner who is 40% owner, and he is managing the business as I have been able to automate that business and step away from running it daily. I've moved on to do more writing, speaking, and encouraging others, and I'm very excited to get to do those things. But the truth is, I was knocked down over and over in this business. I could write a whole other book just about the things that happened with this business alone.

The Adversity of a Health Crisis:

I wasn't kidding when I said I understood adversity. As if being married to a con man and having all the business struggles I'd had weren't enough, life threw me a diagnosis four years prior to writing this that resulted in doctors telling me, "You only have a year to live." Up until then, I had been an extremely healthy person. In my mid-forties at this time and experiencing some weird symptoms, I finally drove myself to the ER one night, telling my husband to just stay home with the kids as they rested and that I'd go get checked out real quick. But I was worse off than I let on and I felt horrible, and to this day, I don't know how I was even able to walk or drive myself in. After almost being discharged and sent home, the doctor luckily (and at the last moment) realized my heart rate was too high to release me. They admitted me and began running more tests. Right there in the ER, they knew something was bad, very bad, but still didn't know what. It wasn't until the next day, after some more testing, that they found my heart was only functioning at 15%. Now, you can drop dead if it's below 35%, so as you can imagine, it was not good. I was told I would be lucky if I lived another year. At one point I nearly crashed and had to be sent to the ICU. While in the ICU, I was told that my only hope may be to get on the heart transplant list.

But I emerged from the darkness of this health scare not only to survive but to thrive. I even still have my own heart. And in doing so, I found my purpose—to learn the lessons I needed to learn and to help YOU overcome adversities so you can thrive too. That is why I am on a mission to motivate you to be what I call a NOISE-maker!

The Adversity of Being Vulnerable:

I only recently began talking publicly about my marriage to a con man for the first time after leaving him 16 years earlier. That's a long time to not talk about something, and I was nervous but, for a number of reasons, I knew it was time for me to share this part of my life. A few months later, I began a podcast called *Let's Make Some Noise.* I talk about turning adversity into positive NOISE, which you now know is my acronym for a Narrative of Inspiration, Strength, and Encouragement. I've discovered a profound strength in exposing my darkest and most embarrassing moments to the world, and that is a journey where embarrassment and silence transformed into freedom and more NOISE for me.

After all this adversity, I hope you are now wondering what this ROCKY WATER approach to life is. Let's get into that now.

ROCKY:

I love boxing, so naturally, the *Rocky* movies are inspiring and moving to me. My grandfather was a golden gloves boxer before joining the Navy during World War II. I even have an old black-and-white photo of him boxing at an exhibition match at Folsom Prison. You know, the prison Johnny Cash sings about? My sisters and I would spend our summers with our grandparents. Grandpa was always very active, even doing his daily stretches and touching his toes when he was over ninety years old. He taught us how to put our stomachs on a basketball and roll back and forth to toughen up our abdominal muscles like he did as a boxer. Growing up, I'd see my dad watching boxing matches on ESPN and always appreciated the focus, strategies, and most importantly, the grit of boxers. I mean, to get punched in the face or ribs, get knocked to the ground, and dare to get right back up knowing it could happen again! That's courage because I know they didn't want to get punched in the face another time. That hurts anyone. I always think of these things when I'm going through hard times: "Just get back up." And just like Rocky in the first movie, you may not even win the match—but you are a winner just by getting up and trying.

I've failed so many times, I've been knocked down a lot, but I kept getting up, and this is where the "ROCKY" portion of my approach comes from. To understand this on a deeper level, I have an acronym for ROCKY:

Reframe your perspective: Look at the situation from different angles to find new solutions. A boxer must know how to pivot quickly, and so will you.

Organize your thoughts: Start with gratefulness. The part of your brain where anxiety about future thoughts resides is the same place where gratitude is found, and they cancel each other out. What an amazing gift to be able to replace those thoughts that create dread with thoughts that create hope.

Connect with others: Seek support from friends, family, or support groups to share your feelings and gain insights. Even if that means reaching out to a therapist.

Keep getting up: Stamina is paramount to winning the fight. Take a shower, put on some fresh clothes, maybe even some lipstick, and earrings—even if you aren't leaving the house, this does wonders!

Yield to self-compassion: Be kind to yourself, acknowledging that setbacks are a natural part of life.

WATER:

This is my favorite thing to talk about. When I was recovering from heart failure (the first time), I had to slow down the work I was doing in my business. It was like reverting to the days when my babies were little and focusing on the business last, for the most part. The difference was, my kids were older and self-reliant, and I had more quiet time to myself. Instead of filling that quiet time with television or more work, I got back into painting, something I hadn't done for 30 years because I had become too busy and I never slowed down enough to pick up a paintbrush. I had only done oil painting in the past, but this time I tried watercolor painting for the first time and fell in love with the art.

One day, I was sitting at my dining table painting, on a quiet afternoon, while still in a health crisis and wearing a defibrillator LifeVest™, and it occurred to me that the difference between oil painting and watercolor painting was huge. With oils, the painter has a lot of control, but with watercolors, the water has control, and as the artist, you must let go and let the water create the beauty which may end up looking different than how you had planned. I began to cry because I related it to my own life. I had to LET GO. I couldn't control where I was in life or my heart issues. I could show up and do what I could do best, but I was not the one with control. For me, God was in control, and I wanted Him to be. I wanted to allow a masterpiece to be created from my life, even if it looked different from how I had originally planned. And that is what I began to do. To understand this on a deeper level, I also have an acronym for WATER:

Welcome imperfection: Embrace your flaws and recognize that nothing is perfect.

Accept uncertainty: Understand that not everything can be controlled, and that's ok.

Trust the process: Have faith that things will work out, even if you can't see the entire path.

Embrace the moment and let go of worries about the future: Anxiety is thinking about the future. Live in the present.

Relinquish expectations: Release the need for things to always go as planned, and be open to surprises and detours in life.

When we go through adversity, like a messy divorce, the death of a family member, health scares, or a traumatic event, it is ok to grieve. That is healthy, important, and physically necessary for our mental health. Our tears have proven this. Tears are a superpower, so use them. Microscopically, scientists can tell the difference between happy, sad, and angry tears. Science has also found that tears eliminate toxins from the body. So I'm not saying, "Suck it up, buttercup, pull up your big girl panties." No, I'm saying grieve, cry, get angry for a bit, just don't stay there for too long. Get back up! It may look like putting your hair in a messy bun and wearing some lipstick, even if you aren't going to leave the house, just because it makes you feel more like you. Or it may look like inviting a friend over for coffee just so you have some personal interaction. It's not a "Fake it 'til you make it." It's a "Do it 'til you feel it." Life has its cycle of seasons just like nature, and I'm saying that I don't want you to hibernate through all the seasons because you didn't pull a *Rocky* and get back up and because you didn't recognize the power of WATER and letting go. Show up, do your part, but let go and let the rest fall into place.

Making NOISE is a call to action—a reminder that our stories have the power to inspire others, to give them the strength to face their challenges, and to encourage them to keep going, even when the road ahead seems daunting.

The ROCKY WATER approach to life allows you to show up and create NOISE from your adversity so that you will be an encouragement to those who know you. Now, go make some NOISE!

P.S. While the main title of this book is *Dare To Dream Big: Scaling, Innovation & Success in Entrepreneurship,* I feel it's important for you to understand that your success is NOT tied to facts such as you creating one of the fastest selling products or building the highest grossing business in your industry, or even building any business at all—maybe entrepreneurship isn't even a desire of yours. That's ok too. My hope is you come away from reading this knowing that your success is instead tied to your willingness to get back up and your willingness to let go so that a beautiful masterpiece can be created from your life, no matter what adversities you face. Don't diminish the success in your life that comes from the ROCKY WATER approach. Use every win as a springboard and encouragement for your next win, and continue to dare to dream big! When another setback comes your way…ROCKY WATER can still be at play.

P.S.S. I have an exciting update that happened toward the end of me writing this book. My heart function is back up and I'm continuing to heal, and I feel great. I already have speaking engagements booked and am so excited to continue being a NOISE-maker myself. If you have an audience in need of a motivational speaker, I'd love it if you kept me in mind. Reach out to see how I can help encourage them. My desire is for everyone to understand the power of the ROCKY WATER approach and use it to become a NOISE-maker themselves. If you read this and it inspired you, please reach out to me and let me know. It will encourage me.

—Edwina The Encourager

JOIN THE MOVEMENT!
#BAUW

Becoming An Unstoppable Woman
With She Rises Studios

She Rises Studios was founded by Hanna Olivas and Adriana Luna Carlos, the mother-daughter duo, in mid-2020 as they saw a need to help empower women worldwide. They are the podcast hosts of the *She Rises Studios Podcast* and Amazon best-selling authors and motivational speakers who travel the world. Hanna and Adriana are the movement creators of #BAUW - Becoming An Unstoppable Woman: The movement has been created to universally impact women of all ages, at whatever stage of life, to overcome insecurities, and adversities, and develop an unstoppable mindset. She Rises Studios educates, celebrates, and empowers women globally.

Looking to Join Us in our Next Anthology or Publish YOUR Own?

She Rises Studios Publishing offers full-service publishing, marketing, book tour, and campaign services. For more information, contact info@sherisesstudios.com

We are always looking for women who want to share their stories and expertise and feature their businesses on our podcasts, in our books, and in our magazines.

SEE WHAT WE DO

OUR PODCAST   OUR BOOKS   OUR SERVICES

Be featured in the Becoming An Unstoppable Woman magazine, published in 13 countries and sold in all major retailers. Get the visibility you need to LEVEL UP in your business!

Have your own TV show streamed across major platforms like Roku TV, Amazon Fire Stick, Apple TV and more!

Learn to leverage your expertise. Build your online presence and grow your audience with FENIX TV.
https://fenixtv.sherisesstudios.com/

Visit www.SheRisesStudios.com to see how YOU can join the #BAUW movement and help your community to achieve the UNSTOPPABLE mindset.

Have you checked out the *She Rises Studios Podcast?*

Find us on all MAJOR platforms: Spotify, IHeartRadio, Apple Podcasts, Google Podcasts, etc.

Looking to become a sponsor or build a partnership?

Email us at info@sherisesstudios.com

www.ingramcontent.com/pod-product-compliance
Lightning Source LLC
Chambersburg PA
CBHW051006140626
46546CB00016B/883